RETRIEV
Ressc
IN CATHOLIC THOUGHT

MW00620565

The middle years of the twentieth century marked a particularly intense time of crisis and change in European society. During this period (1930-1950), a broad intellectual and spiritual movement arose within the European Catholic community, largely in response to the secularism that lay at the core of the crisis. The movement drew inspiration from earlier theologians and philosophers such as Möhler, Newman, Gardeil, Rousselot, and Blondel, as well as from men of letters like Charles Péguy and Paul Claudel.

The group of academic theologians included in the movement extended into Belgium and Germany, in the work of men like Emile Mersch, Dom Odo Casel, Romano Guardini, and Karl Adam. But above all the theological activity during this period centered in France. Led principally by the Jesuits at Fourvière and the Dominicans at Le Saulchoir, the French revival included many of the greatest names in twentieth-century Catholic thought: Henri de Lubac, Jean Daniélou, Yves Congar, Marie-Dominique Chenu, Louis Bouyer, and, in association, Hans Urs von Balthasar.

It is not true — as subsequent folklore has it — that those theologians represented any sort of self-conscious "school": indeed, the differences among them, for example, between Fourvière and Saulchoir, were important. At the same time, most of them were united in the double conviction that theology had to speak to the present situation, and that the condition for doing so faithfully lay in a recovery of the Church's past. In other words, they saw clearly that the first step in what later came to be known as *aggiornamento* had to be *ressourcement* — a rediscovery of the riches of the whole of the Church's two-thousand-year tradition. According to de Lubac, for example, all of his own works as well as the entire *Sources chrétiennes* collection are based on the presupposition that "the renewal of Christian vitality is linked at least partially to a renewed exploration of the periods and of the works where the Christian tradition is expressed with particular intensity."

In sum, for the *ressourcement* theologians theology involved a "return to the sources" of Christian faith, for the purpose of drawing out the meaning and significance of these sources for the critical questions of our time. What these theologians sought was a spiritual and intellectual communion with Christianity in its most vital moments as transmitted to us in its classic texts, a communion that would nourish, invigorate, and rejuvenate twentieth-century Catholicism.

The *ressourcement* movement bore great fruit in the documents of the Second Vatican Council and deeply influenced the work of Pope John Paul II.

The present series is rooted in this renewal of theology. The series thus understands *ressourcement* as revitalization: a return to the sources, for the purpose of developing a theology that will truly meet the challenges of our time. Some of the features of the series, then, are a return to classical (patristic-medieval) sources and a dialogue with contemporary Western culture, particularly in terms of problems associated with the Enlightenment, modernity, and liberalism.

The series publishes out-of-print or as yet untranslated studies by earlier authors associated with the *ressourcement* movement. The series also publishes works by contemporary authors sharing in the aim and spirit of this earlier movement. This will include any works in theology, philosophy, history, literature, and the arts that give renewed expression to Catholic sensibility.

The editor of the Ressourcement series, David L. Schindler, is Gagnon Professor of Fundamental Theology and dean at the John Paul II Institute in Washington, D.C., and editor of the North American edition of *Communio: International Catholic Review*, a federation of journals in thirteen countries founded in Europe in 1972 by Hans Urs von Balthasar, Jean Daniélou, Henri de Lubac, Joseph Ratzinger, and others.

RETRIEVAL & RENEWAL

IN CATHOLIC THOUGHT

VOLUMES PUBLISHED

Mysterium Paschale
Hans Urs von Balthasar

The Heroic Face of Innocence: Three Stories
Georges Bernanos

The Letter on Apologetics and *History and Dogma*
Maurice Blondel

Prayer: The Mission of the Church
Jean Daniélou

On Pilgrimage
Dorothy Day

We, the Ordinary People of the Streets
Madeleine Delbrêl

The Discovery of God
Henri de Lubac

Medieval Exegesis, volumes 1 and 2:
The Four Senses of Scripture
Henri de Lubac

Opening Up the Scriptures:
Joseph Ratzinger and the Foundations of Biblical Interpretation
José Granados, Carlos Granados, and Luis Sánchez-Navarro, eds.

Letters from Lake Como:
Explorations in Technology and the Human Race
Romano Guardini

Divine Likeness: Toward a Trinitarian Anthropology of the Family
Marc Cardinal Ouellet

The Portal of the Mystery of Hope
Charles Péguy

In the Beginning:
A Catholic Understanding of the Story of Creation and the Fall
Joseph Cardinal Ratzinger

In the Fire of the Burning Bush:
An Initiation to the Spiritual Life
Marko Ivan Rupnik

Love Alone Is Credible:
Hans Urs von Balthasar as Interpreter
of the Catholic Tradition, volume I
David L. Schindler, ed.

Hans Urs von Balthasar: A Theological Style
Angelo Scola

The Nuptial Mystery
Angelo Scola

Opening Up the Scriptures

Joseph Ratzinger and the Foundations
of Biblical Interpretation

Edited by

José Granados

Carlos Granados

&

Luis Sánchez-Navarro

WILLIAM B. EERDMANS PUBLISHING COMPANY

GRAND RAPIDS, MICHIGAN / CAMBRIDGE, U.K.

Originally published as
Escritura e interpretación. Los fundamentos de la interpretación bíblica,
edited by Luis Sánchez-Navarro and Carlos Granados
(Madrid, Ediciones Palabra, 2003)

Published 2008 by
Wm. B. Eerdmans Publishing Co.
2140 Oak Industrial Drive N.E., Grand Rapids, Michigan 49505 /
P.O. Box 163, Cambridge CB3 9PU U.K.

Printed in the United States of America

14 13 12 11 10 09   7 6 5 4 3 2

Library of Congress Cataloging-in-Publication Data

Escritura e interpretación. English.
Opening up the Scriptures: Joseph Ratzinger and the foundations of biblical interpretation /
edited by José Granados, Carlos Granados & Luis Sánchez-Navarro.
p.   cm.   — (Ressourcement : retrieval and renewal in Catholic thought)
Includes bibliographical references and indexes.
ISBN 978-0-8028-6011-8 (pbk.: alk. paper)
1. Bible — Hermeneutics.   I. Granados, José.   II. Granados, Carlos.
III. Sánchez-Navarro, Luis, 1965-   IV. Title.

BS476.E7613   2008
220.601 — dc22

2008011045

www.eerdmans.com

Contents

Contents

Contents

Contents

Abbreviations

Biblical books are cited according to the
norms of the *Catholic Biblical Quarterly*

ATD	Das Alte Testament Deutsch (Göttingen)
BBB	Bonner biblische Beiträge (Bonn)
BEB	Biblioteca de estudios bíblicos (Salamanca)
BEThL	Bibliotheca ephemeridum theologicarum Lovaniensium (Louvain)
Bib	*Biblica* (Rome)
BK	Biblischer Kommentar. Altes Testament (Neukirchen-Vluyn)
BLitE	*Bulletin de littérature ecclésiastique* (Toulouse)
CCC	*Catechism of the Catholic Church*, Vatican City-Washington, D.C.: Libreria Editrice Vaticana-United States Catholic Conference, ²2000
CCL	Corpus Christianorum. Series Latina (Turnhout)
CEFR	Collection de l'École française de Rome (Rome)
ChW	*Christliche Welt* (Marburg)
Communio.de	*Communio*. Internationale katholische Zeitschrift (Freiburg)
Communio.en	*Communio*. International Catholic Review (Washington)

Communio.fr	*Communio*. Revue catholique international (Paris)
Concilium	*Concilium*. Revista internacional de Teología (Madrid)
DAS	*Divino Afflante Spiritu*, Encyclical of Pope Pius XII promoting biblical studies (1943)
DH	H. Denzinger — P. Hünermann, *Kompendium der Glaubensbekenntnisse und kirchlichen Lehrentscheidungen*, Freiburg: Herder, 2005.
DV	Dogmatic Constitution *Dei Verbum* on Divine Revelation (Vatican II, 1965).
EB	*Enchiridion biblicum. Documenti della Chiesa sulla Sacra Scrittura*, Bologna: Dehoniane, ³2004
EstBíb	*Estudios bíblicos* (Madrid)
EstEcl	*Estudios eclesiásticos* (Madrid)
GAT	Grundrisse zum Alten Testament (Göttingen)
GNT	Grundrisse zum Neuen Testament (Göttingen)
GS	Pastoral Constitution *Gaudium et spes* on the Church in the Modern World (Vatican II, 1965)
Int	*Interpretation* (Richmond, VA)
Laur	*Laurentianum* (Brindisi)
LG	Dogmatic Constitution *Lumen Gentium* on the Church (Vatican II, 1964)
LP	Libros Palabra (Madrid)
LThK	J. Höfer — K. Rahner (ed.), *Lexikon für Theologie und Kirche*, Freiburg: Herder, 1957-1967
MThZ	*Münchener theologische Zeitschrift* (München)
NRT	*Nouvelle revue théologique* (Louvain)
OBO	Orbis biblicus et orientalis (Fribourg)
OTL	Old Testament Library
PG	J. Migne, Patrologia Graeca (Paris)
PL	J. Migne, Patrologia Latina (Paris)
PT	Presencia teológica (Santander)
QD	Quaestiones disputatae (Freiburg)
RHE	*Revue d'histoire ecclésiastique* (Louvain)
RQ	*Römische Quartalschrift für christliche Altertumskunde und Kirchengeschichte* (Freiburg)

RThL	*Revue théologique de Louvain* (Louvain)
SBAW.PH	Sitzungsberichte der Bayerischen Akademie der Wissenschaften. Philosophisch-historische Klasse (München)
SC	Sources chrétiennes (Paris)
Sem	*Seminarium* (Vatican City)
StPat	*Studia Patavina* (Padova)
TDNT	G. Kittel — G. Friedrich (ed.), *Theological Dictionary of the New Testament*, vols. I-X, Grand Rapids: Eerdmans, 1964-1976
TDOT	G. J. Botterweck — H. Ringgren (ed.), *Theological Dictionary of the Old Testament*, vols. I-XIV, Grand Rapids: Eerdmans, 1977-2004
ThBer	Theologische Berichte (Zürich)
ThBüch	Theologische Bücherei (München)
ThDiss	Theologische Dissertationen (Basel)
ThG	*Theologie der Gegenwart* (Würzburg)
ThQ	*Theologische Quartalschrift* (Tübingen)
ThRev	*Theologische Revue* (Münster)
TThZ	*Trierer theologische Zeitschrift* (Mainz)
VTS	Supplements to *Vetus Testamentum* (Leiden)
ZAW	*Zeitschrift für die alttestamentliche Wissenschaft* (Berlin)

Preface to the American Edition

José Granados

In 1988, then-Cardinal Joseph Ratzinger attended a conference in New York, where he presented a lecture on the crisis of biblical interpretation and other scholars offered complementary viewpoints. The proceedings of the conference were published the following year by Richard John Neuhaus under the title, *Biblical Interpretation in Crisis: The Ratzinger Conference on Bible and Church.*[1] The main topic of Ratzinger's presentation was the necessity of submitting the historical-critical method to a thorough revision, what he termed a criticism of the criticism. Raymond Brown, for his part, presented an essay that insisted rather on the positive fruits the historical-critical method has yielded.[2]

Along with two other papers by George Lindbeck and William H. Lazareth, the published conference proceedings also included a text on the discussion that followed the presentations among the twenty or so partici-

1. Grand Rapids: Eerdmans, 1989.
2. "The Contribution of Historical Biblical Criticism to Ecumenical Church Discussion," in *Biblical Interpretation in Crisis,* pp. 24-49.

Fr. José Granados (Madrid 1970), Disciple of the Hearts of Jesus and Mary, holds a doctorate in Sacred Theology (Gregorian Pontifical University, Rome, 2005). He is Assistant Professor of Theology at the John Paul II Institute for Studies on Marriage and Family at The Catholic University of America.

pating scholars.[3] In the course of this conversation, Cardinal Ratzinger summarized his proposal as follows: If we call patristic and medieval exegesis "method A" and the historical-critical exegesis "method B," we need to find a new method ("method C") that would take into account the advantages of these two approaches and would also be able to overcome their limits.[4] The task of developing this new method C, according to Ratzinger, will take the work of an entire generation.

Raymond Brown offered his own viewpoint on the critique of the method. In his opinion, Ratzinger's presentation reflected a pessimistic view of the historical-critical approach based on the way its implementation had occurred in the Cardinal's own European environment. In this regard, the European scene was quite different from the American one. Many American scholars, in using the historical-critical method, were well aware that it was not the only tool for understanding the text. They know that, once the method had arrived at its conclusions, there remained many unanswered questions; at this point it was precisely the role of the teaching Church and of theological reflection, both informed by the Bible, to go beyond the Bible.

What Brown's contribution failed to grasp, however, was that Ratzinger's comments were directed not so much at the way the scholars use the method as at the method itself, inasmuch as it entails distinctive presuppositions that bear on its findings. The main problem is that the method allows the teaching Church and theological reflection to go "beyond" its results only "after" it has finished its analysis. But then any kind of ecclesial exegesis that rejects the need for a radical reform of the historical-critical approach would introduce the point of view of faith only after completion of the textual analysis. Church and theology, then, will always be latecomers to the conversation and will have something to contribute only if there is some remaining question, or some issue for which no conclusion has been reached. A criticism of the criticism is, thus, not solely a European problem, but rather affects the common ground itself in which

---

3. "The Story of an Encounter," by Paul T. Stallsworth, in *Biblical Interpretation in Crisis*, pp. 102-90.

4. Cf. "The Story of an Encounter," pp. 107-8.

exegesis is practiced; this is why it is the method itself, and not the mind-set of the scholar who uses it, that needs to undergo a thorough revision.

George Lindbeck's paper, "Scripture, Consensus and Community," of-fers another American perspective.[5] Lindbeck pointed out the progress of biblical interpretation in the Anglo-Saxon world as a result of the narrative consideration of the text. Approaching the text as a story prevents its frag-mentation into isolated units and allows an interpretation of the Bible as a whole, while also taking into account the interrelationship between the Old and the New Testaments. Yet two questions remained and were discussed in the subsequent conversation: What is the connection between the narra-tive of the text and the factuality of the events of history? If the story nar-rated by the text is self-referential, in what sense does it stand in need of an ecclesial interpretation?

The present book offers the complete text (in a new translation of the German original, which was published in 1989) of the lecture originally given by Cardinal Ratzinger in New York, but within a different setting from the original American context in which it was delivered and pub-lished. Ratzinger's remarks on the historical-critical method are sur-rounded now by different voices, this time from a Continental milieu. Here, exegetes of great renown and influence on the European scene dur-ing the years following the Second Vatican Council, such as I. de la Potterie, K. Stock, A. Vanhoye, B. Costacurta, and P. Beauchamp, reflect specifically on the question posed by Ratzinger at the New York confer-ence and offer a precious contribution to the original discussion.

All of the contributors accept that the critique of the method not only calls the exegete to a different way of thinking, that is, a purification of his intention when dealing with the method, but also requires a new under-standing of the method itself. Acknowledging that the elements for a syn-thesis are already present, they intend to offer proposals for combining these elements in a fruitful manner.

The method needs to be open, first of all, to the hermeneutical ques-tion. Paul Beauchamp, whom Paul Ricoeur once called "an explorer of the Bible . . . who dedicated himself to *think the Bible*," reminds us of the need

---

5. In *Biblical Interpretation in Crisis*, pp. 74-101.

to develop a philosophy of the narrative act, thus connecting with Lindbeck's concerns. The philosophical question about the meaning of a text, about the story it conveys and its relationship with historiography, is at the basis of developing "method C." This question must now proceed to the more fundamental one of the relationship between word and event, realizing that there is meaning in historical reality and in the natural world even before any written or oral expression.

Viewed in this light, the exegetical problem appears to be a particular case of a more general one: the problem of the relationship between science, on the one hand, and philosophy and theology, on the other. After all, the historical-critical method describes itself as purely scientific, i.e., able to achieve results that are totally independent from the scientist's point of view, with an accuracy that has no need of further interpretation. The method thus claims for itself the autonomy and independence of the other natural sciences. But this claim, which was understandable enough a hundred years ago, is no longer sustainable. Science itself has realized the necessity of being open to the complexity of reality and of abandoning its claims of total certainty as to its conclusions.

The very openness to the hermeneutical question would help to open the method to the question of faith, as well. The two elements that were set forth by the Second Vatican Council's constitution *Dei Verbum*, the point of view of faith and the intention of the human author, could then be seen in their proper integration. Cardinal A. Vanhoye offers interesting reflections in this regard in his contribution to this volume.

In the final article of this book, Cardinal Ratzinger deals specifically with the relationship between the Magisterium and exegesis, once again offering fresh reflections on how the synthesis can be achieved. Only if the critical method is able to open itself, to redefine its presuppositions, will it be possible for the voice of the Church to enter in as an internal part of the method, and not merely as something superadded that can only arrive too late for the given interpretation. The elements of truth that the historical-critical method uncovers, the valid concerns it brings to exegesis, will certainly remain, but their interrelationship will change as these are taken up into a new dynamism.

Cardinal Ratzinger refers, in his latter contribution, to the Promised

Land of freedom that Catholic exegetes dreamt of at the beginning of the last century, a freedom understood as deliverance from the limitations of Church teaching. But freedom, if it is to be real, is not self-sufficient autonomy. On the contrary, it remains always open to surprise, to a transformation that comes from beyond ourselves and helps us to comprehend the past and to be open to the future.[6] As long as any critical method disallows the living character of the text, and the text's own capacity for transcendence, its freedom can only be an impoverished one, not the authentic freedom spoken of by the Bible itself. It is on behalf of this freedom that this collection of essays would like to speak and offer its own contribution.

I would like to express my gratitude to Lesley Rice for her help in editing the manuscript.

---

6. Cf. P. Ricoeur, "Freedom in the Light of Hope," in *The Conflict of Interpretations: Essays in Hermeneutics* (London: Northwestern University Press, 1989), pp. 402-24.

On the Horizon of Hope

CARLOS GRANADOS and LUIS SÁNCHEZ-NAVARRO

The interpretation of Sacred Scripture is a topic of perennial interest for the Church. The written Word of God constitutes "the strength of faith for the Church's sons and daughters, the nourishment for their souls, the pure and everlasting source of spiritual life" (DV 21). The history of the Church is, to a large extent, the history of the understanding and experience of the revealed deposit, to which Sacred Scripture, inspired by God, offers an authentic witness. Every generation of Christians has centered its attention on the sacred books, eager to deepen in faith and to mature in the Christian life. To this end our era is also called, at the dawn of the twenty-first century, and it is because of this mission that biblical exegesis possesses an ecclesial significance of the highest order.

Fr. Carlos Granados (Madrid 1974), Disciple of the Hearts of Jesus and Mary, holds a licentiate in Sacred Scripture (Pontifical Biblical Institute, Rome, 2004). A member of the Spanish Biblical Association, he is presently completing his doctoral dissertation at the Biblical Institute. Fr. Luis Sánchez-Navarro (Madrid 1965), from the same religious Institute, holds a doctorate in Greek philology (Complutense University, Madrid, 1995) and in Sacred Scripture (Pontifical Biblical Institute, Rome, 2004). A member of the Spanish Biblical Association and of the Catholic Biblical Association of America, he is at present a professor of Sacred Scripture at the "San Dámaso" Theological Faculty (Madrid) and at the John Paul II Institute for Studies on Marriage and Family at the Catholic University of America.

Contemporary exegesis does not begin indiscriminately, for we are indebted to a history that is both long and enriching. However, its various phases echo a complex question which, in the wake of the "revolution" experienced by European culture during the Enlightenment, we can pose in the following manner: What is the proper understanding of Scripture? Or said in another way: Is biblical interpretation feasible while remaining on faith's periphery? The literary character of the biblical writings, which corresponds to the logic of the Incarnation, obliges us to clarify its historical and philological aspects. This, in turn, demands a comparative study with other works from antiquity. Yet, does this suffice? A brief look at the last century will shed light on this fundamental question.

Vatican Council II's dogmatic constitution *Dei Verbum*, on divine Revelation (1965), appeared as a milestone after almost a century of scholarship and trial endeavors in the Catholic milieu regarding the interpretation of Scripture. Following the encyclical *Providentissimus Deus* (1893), in which Leo XIII encouraged and advocated Sacred Scripture studies; after the vicissitudes of the modernist era and the favorable openness created by the encyclical *Divino Afflante Spiritu* of Pius XII (1943), DV 11-12 set forth the questions relating to the inspiration and interpretation of Sacred Scripture. It incorporated the advancements of modern exegetical science from within the traditional Christian understanding, recognizing here the written testimony of the Word of God. Thus a fruitful path opened up for research on the "Book of all books," that is, on the Bible.

This path has been trod by many who have demonstrated the fruitfulness stemming from the Council's teachings. In particular, the study of Sacred Scripture according to the historical method has allowed for a better understanding of its literary beginnings. The birth of historical studies as well as the twentieth-century archaeological discoveries, which have cast an intense light upon the biblical writings (the most noteworthy case being Qumran), have contributed to a greater development of this approach.

This attentive eye to history is and will continue to be indispensable to exegetical efforts, for what characterizes biblical exegesis with respect to the other theological disciplines is its particular consideration of the *textual mediation* of the Word of God. This, in turn, requires a unique background of linguistic, literary, and historical knowledge. Still, in the past few decades one can discover — and not only within Catholic circles — a growing uneasiness with respect to the exclusive use of the historical-critical method. The latter tends to overshadow the supernatural element present in the biblical texts, not infrequently proffering its conclusions as the only and definitive explanation for the texts.[1] On a practical level, this has led to a distancing of a few believers from Scripture, which, as it is relegated to the past, is perceived as a reality inconsequential for the life of faith.

For this reason, a critical reflection on the foundations of biblical interpretation has been recognized as an imperative task: a reflection that, in keeping with Vatican II, must combine study of the sacred text according to the human sciences with a method of study that is specifically "biblical." In other words, the methodology must be located within the framework of the entire Bible and clarified by means of its relationship with the Old and New Testaments in order to show — by the light of faith — its theological meaning inasmuch as it is a written testimony of the revelation of God.[2] Therefore, critical reflection regarding the foundations, scope, and limits of the historical-critical method is necessary, and will, in turn, allow for fruitful advancements in biblical studies.

The desire to encourage this reflection has prompted us to offer to the English-speaking public the writings that make up this collection. The contributions that we present here bear witness to that demand for a critical reexamination of these methods; there is a need in biblical studies for what K. Stock calls an "ecological revolution" that respects the specific characteristics of these texts, without forcibly imposing criteria or expectations that are foreign to them. In this way, one attempts to overcome excesses, both critical (historicism) and ideological (materialism, feminism, psychologism), at one extreme, and fundamentalist, at the other. One thus seeks to integrate scientific biblical exegesis into the ecclesial context to which it belongs, thereby avoiding a separation between exegesis and interpretation — terms that, in the conciliar text, indicate the same reality.

The fundamental presupposition upon which biblical exegesis is based

1. An important work from an ecumenical perspective is C. E. Braaten and R. W. Jenson, eds., *Reclaiming the Bible for the Church* (Edinburgh: T. & T. Clark, 1996).

2. See L. Sánchez-Navarro, "The Testimonial Character of Sacred Scripture," *Communio.en* 30 (2003): 320-36.

is the Bible's unity; conforming to this requires of the exegete, in the words of B. Costacurta, an authentic "hermeneutical decision." By saying *the Bible*, in singular (let us not forget that in Greek *biblía* is plural, "books"), we are already implying that it is a question of a plurality with a unity in meaning, a unity that is found precisely in its overall context. Its subject (the people of Israel who achieve their fullness in the Church), the reality to which it testifies (the revelation of God in history), and its distinctive quality (divine inspiration) all confer a unified character that is deeper than the literary and historical dissimilarities. The authors who have collaborated in this volume, each one according to his own style and particular approach, heavily stress this essential aspect.

*   *   *

In the first essay, whose impact within the field of biblical studies has been and continues to be extensive, Cardinal Joseph Ratzinger[3] speaks of the need for a "self-criticism of the historical method."[4] Herein lies the Cardinal's foremost contribution to this debate: what is needed is a "criticism of the criticism" carried out *from within the criticism itself,* making use of its own potential, and that extends to a critique of historical reason. It is necessary to review the results that have been achieved up until now, and bring to light the suppositions on which they depend to a large extent; thus the debate is proposed on a philosophical level. Moreover, one must take into account that the interpretation of Scripture is not a historical science, but rather a hermeneutical one that points to the meaning of the biblical texts as they relate to God's revelation.

3. Marktl am Inn (Germany), 1927. Professor of Theology at the universities of Bonn (1959), Münster (1963), Tübingen (1966), and Regensburg (1969). He was archbishop of Munich (1977-1981) and prefect of the Congregation for the Doctrine of the Faith and president of the Pontifical Biblical Commission (1981-2005). On April 19, 2005, he was elected Pope, taking the name Benedict XVI.

4. This paper, given in New York on January 27, 1988, has been published in German and translated into Italian, French, English, and Spanish. For the original publications and translations into other languages of all the contributions contained in this volume, see pp. 137-38.

Along with the full English version of this conference[5] there are some writings concerning the hermeneutical foundations for exegesis, the work of notable, contemporary Catholic exegetes. These writings attest to the relevance of Cardinal Ratzinger's reflections in addition to pointing out a path to follow from within exegetical science itself.

In his significant contribution, Ignace de la Potterie[6] takes up an expression from Romano Guardini, who defined biblical exegesis as the "science of faith." In other words, it is a scientific discipline of a theological nature. In what he himself calls his "academic testament,"[7] de la Potterie shows how interpreting the biblical text means going beyond the text itself until one reaches its greatest depth, its revelatory *meaning*. Worthy of mention, apart from the philosophical interest these reflections contain, are de la Potterie's foundations in biblical exegesis and in the best exponents from the ecclesial tradition, as well as his consideration for recent advancements in hermeneutics.

The article by Paul Beauchamp[8] can also be regarded as a synthesis that illustrates the principal interest that has given impetus to his academic life and scholarly work: the building of a "biblical theology," understood as that reflection that illustrates the relationship and the break between "one Testament and the other" and discovers their principles. In keeping with the profound intuition that distinguishes him, Beauchamp sets forth the necessary conditions so as to move ahead towards such an undertaking.

The brief and delightful contribution from Bruna Costacurta[9] insists

---

5. The English translation published in 1989 was shorter than the original German; in this volume, we present an unabridged version.

6. Waregem (Belgium), 1914–Heverlee (Belgium), 2003. He was professor of New Testament at Louvain (1950-1960) and at the Pontifical Biblical Institute in Rome (1960-1989).

7. Here is reproduced an augmented version of the text of the paper given at the Pontifical Biblical Institute on December 15, 1989, on the occasion of his being named professor emeritus.

8. Tours (France), 1924–Paris, 2001. He was professor of Old Testament at the Faculty of Fontaines (Chantilly: 1960-62), at the Pontifical Biblical Institute (1962-64), at the Faculty of Fourvière (Lyon: 1965-74), of which he was dean from 1966 until 1972, and at the Centre Sèvres (Paris: 1974-94).

9. Rome, 1946. Since 1978, she has been professor of Old Testament at the Pontifical

on the principles already put forth, upon which she expounds through an insightful and original interpretation of Genesis 2–3. Here she shows how, in order to attain the true meaning of the texts, it is essential that one consider the text in its canonical form (which we might say is its only *real* form), confronting the difficulties rather than omitting them. One must accept them and discover a source of meaning in the (perhaps only apparent) contradictions within the text.

In "Christ in Contemporary Exegesis," Klemens Stock,[10] after a reasoned *status quaestionis* concerning the present situation of New Testament exegesis, indicates the path the latter should follow in order to grasp the message of the gospels in all its profundity, especially the figure of Christ. To this end, he presents the gospel writings as the inseparable outcome of "what Jesus did in word and deed" (*Wirken Jesu*) and of the "effect Jesus had" (*Wirkung Jesu*) on the witnesses chosen by him to convey his message. The specific character of the gospels, in which the words of Jesus and those of the evangelists cannot be dissociated, is not then an obstacle to gaining access to the real and complete Jesus, but rather the most suitable means for achieving this.

The collaborative efforts of Albert Vanhoye[11] deal with the reception of the constitution *Dei Verbum* in the Church. The overall scene is hopeful, though still not without problematic areas (such as the reduction of the Word of God to Scripture and the underestimation of Tradition); biblical studies are a promising reality today. This promise depends, however, on biblical scholars' ability to assume an appropriate hermeneutic viewpoint

---

Gregorian University (Rome), first in the Institute of Religious Sciences and afterwards in the Faculty of Theology.

10. Aalen-Hofen (Germany), 1934. Professor of New Testament since 1974 at the Pontifical Biblical Institute, of which he was dean (1989-90) and rector (1990-96); since 2002, he has been secretary of the Pontifical Biblical Commission. Between 1978 and 1987 he also taught at Innsbruck.

11. Hazebrouck (France), 1923. Teacher in Chantilly from 1959 to 1962, he is presently professor emeritus of New Testament at the Pontifical Biblical Institute, where he has taught since 1962 and of which he was both dean (1969-75) and rector (1984-90); he has also been president of the *Studiorum Novi Testamenti Societas* (1995) and secretary of the Pontifical Biblical Commission (1993-2001). In March of 2006 he was made Cardinal.

that takes into account its theological character, its ecclesial context, and the unity of all of Scripture.

As a final addition, we have included the paper given in Rome by Cardinal Ratzinger on May 2, 2003, on the occasion of the centenary of the Pontifical Biblical Commission, an institution established by Leo XIII in 1902 through his apostolic letter *Vigilantiae studiique* (EB 137-48) for the promotion of biblical studies. The Cardinal offers us a retrospective look in which his personal history intertwines with the history of this institution and with the course of biblical exegesis in the twentieth century. He proposes a calm acceptance of this history, without quickly condemning the past, seeing it instead as a necessary element in an ongoing process of knowing. In this way, an ever more fruitful research into Sacred Scripture will be possible.

*   *   *

Describing the challenge that confronts contemporary exegesis, which needs to incorporate the achievements of the historical method into a proper hermeneutics, Cardinal Ratzinger said in his essay of 1988: "The work of at least a whole generation is necessary to achieve such a thing." Even now there remains much to do; yet, just as the contributions offered in this volume propose, the horizon that opens up before us sets us closer to this goal than we were twenty years ago. This is why these words represent not a paralyzing obstacle but an incentive and a basis for hope.

Washington, DC, 30 September 2006
Feast of St. Jerome

Translated by Jeff Lawrence

Biblical Interpretation in Conflict:
On the Foundations and the Itinerary of Exegesis Today

Joseph Cardinal Ratzinger

Preliminary Consideration:
Where We Are and What We Must Do

The State of the Problem

In Vladimir Solovyov's *Tale of the Antichrist,* one of the chief strategies by which the eschatological adversary of the Redeemer seeks to ingratiate himself with the faithful is to point out that he has earned a doctorate in theology from Tübingen and that he has written what the experts acknowledge as a pioneering exegetical work. The Antichrist as a famous exegete! Almost a hundred years ago, Solovyov used this paradox to expose the ambivalence of modern methods of interpreting the Bible. Today it has become almost a truism to speak of the crisis of the historical-critical method. And yet, its career began with such boundless optimism.

In the new climate of free thought that the Enlightenment had pioneered, dogma appeared to be the real obstacle to the proper understanding of the Bible on its own terms. Liberated from this biased assumption, and fitted out with methodological equipment that guaranteed strict objectivity, we now seemed at last able to hear anew the voice of the origin, pure and unadulterated. And the fact was that much that had been long forgotten emerged once again to the forefront; it became possible to hear

1

once more the polyphony of history behind the monotony of traditional interpretation. Because the human factor in sacred history came more and more vividly to light, God's action also revealed itself to be grander and nearer than had been supposed. But the picture gradually became more confused. The hypotheses ramified, replaced one another, and under our very eyes became a wall forbidding the uninitiated access to the Bible. The initiated, however, no longer even read the Bible, but break it down into the elements from which it supposedly originated. The method itself seems to require these radical approaches: it cannot stop at some arbitrary point in its attempt to get to the bottom of the human process behind sacred history. It must endeavor to remove the residue of irrationality and to explain everything. Faith is not a component of the method and God is not a factor that it reckons with in historical events. But because the biblical account of history is saturated with divine action, a complicated anatomy of the biblical Word has to be set in motion. It becomes necessary to try to unravel the threads, so that we are left holding the "real history," that is, the purely human side of the events recounted, while also explaining how it is that the idea of God came to be interwoven throughout the text. In other words, we must construct an alternative, "real" history in place of the one the Bible actually recounts; we must find behind the sources that actually exist — the biblical books — other sources that then become the measure of interpretation. It can come as no surprise that, with the application of this procedure, hypotheses have proliferated to the point of becoming a jungle full of contradictions. In the end, one no longer learns what the text says, but what it ought to say, and what components it can be reduced to.[1]

Inevitably, a situation like this has given rise to counter-reactions. Cau-

---

1. C. S. Lewis describes this situation with refreshing directness and great understanding of literature in C. S. Lewis, *Fern Seed and Elephants and Other Essays on Christianity*, ed. W. Hooper (London: Fontana-Collins, 1975). For reflections on the problem based on extensive knowledge of the issues involved, see also E. Kästner, *Die Stundentrommel vom heiligen Berg Athos* (Wiesbaden: Inselverlag, 1956). Also important for the diagnosis of the situation is J. Guitton, *Silence sur l'essentiel* (Paris: Desclée de Brouwer, 1986), pp. 47-58. A useful survey of the history of the historical-critical method can be found in W. Kümmel, *Das Neue Testament. Geschichte der Erforschung seiner Probleme* (Freiburg: Karl Alber, [2]1970).

tious systematicians welcome the prospect of a theology that is as independent as possible from exegesis.[2] But what good can a theology be when it detaches itself from its own foundations? As a result, the radical approach termed "fundamentalism" garners adherents, who characterize the application of historical methods to God's Word as itself false and absurd, and want to get back to listening to the Bible in its pure literality, just as it stands written and as the average hearer understands it. But when do I actually hear the Bible "literally" in the first place? And how do I identify the "normal" understanding that perfectly respects the Bible's specificity? Certainly, fundamentalism can appeal to the fact that the standpoint of the Bible, its own hermeneutical perspective of choice, is how the "little ones," the men of "simple heart," see things.[3] Nevertheless, the fact remains that the demand for "literalness" and "realism" is not at all so clear-cut as it appears.

Another possible way out of the difficulty seems to lie in engagement with the problem of hermeneutics: the explanation of how historical genesis takes place is, we are told, only one part of the exegete's task; the other is to understand the text in today's horizon. Accordingly, we supposedly must investigate the conditions of understanding and thus bring the text into the present in a way that goes beyond the historical "anatomy of the dead."[4] This is correct so far as it goes, for it is true that one is still far from understanding a text simply because one knows how to explain the process of its origination. But how are we to arrive at an understanding that does not rest on arbitrary stipulations of our own, but enables me to hear the message of the text and gives me something other than what I derive from

2. A good example on the Protestant side is P. Tillich, *Systematische Theologie* (Evangelisches Verlagswerk, Stuttgart 1956/58/66) [*Systematic Theology* (Chicago: University of Chicago Press, 1967)], whose index of biblical passages for all three volumes — and this is not an accident — barely takes up two pages. A good example on the Catholic side is the late K. Rahner, who made it a point to keep at least his *Foundations of Christian Faith: An Introduction to the Idea of Christianity* (New York: Seabury Press, 1978) as independent as possible from exegesis (see, for example, p. 14).

3. See J. Guitton, *Silence*, pp. 56ff. R. Guardini, *Das Christusbild der paulinischen und johanneischen Schriften* (Würzburg: Werkbund, [2]1961), p. 15.

4. This formulation comes from Kästner, *Die Stundentrommel*, p. 121; related reflections can be found in L. Kolakowski, *Die Gegenwärtigkeit des Mythos* (München, 1973) [*The Presence of Myth* (Chicago: University of Chicago Press, 1989)], pp. 95f.

myself? Once the method has anatomized history to death, who can resurrect it, giving it the power to speak to me as a living force? Put another way, if "hermeneutics" is going to be convincing, it is necessary to discover the intrinsic concord between historical analysis and hermeneutical synthesis.

I am not questioning, of course, that the discussion surrounding hermeneutics has produced some serious efforts in this direction. I have yet to see a convincing solution, however.[5] Bultmann's deployment of Heidegger's philosophy as a vehicle for bringing the biblical Word into the present was of a piece with his reconstruction of what he took to be the distinctive content of Jesus' message. But was not this reconstruction itself already a product of his philosophy? How credible is it from a historical point of view? Whose voice are we ultimately listening to with this kind of understanding — Jesus' or Heidegger's? Still, we have to recognize that Bultmann was at least seriously struggling to make the message of the Bible accessible.

Today, by contrast, we are beginning to see forms of exegesis that can only be called symptoms of the disintegration of interpretation and hermeneutics. Materialist or feminist interpretation of the Bible cannot seriously claim to be an understanding of the text and its intentions. They are at best an expression of the fact that we regard the real meaning of the Bible either as completely unknowable or as irrelevant to the reality of life today and so no longer ask what is true, but what serves a given form of praxis. The combination of such praxis with elements of the biblical tradition is then justified by the fact that the influx of religious elements enhances the dynamism of action. The historical method can then even serve as a cover for

5. The works of P. Ricoeur merit special mention here, for example, *The Conflict of Interpretations: Essays in Hermeneutics* (Evanston, IL: Northwestern University Press, 1974). P. Stuhlmacher offers a helpful survey in *Vom Verstehen des Neuen Testaments. Eine Hermeneutik* (Göttingen: Vandenhoeck & Ruprecht, 1986). Important first steps can also be found in P. Toinet, *Pour une théologie de l'exégèse* (with a preface by Ignace de la Potterie) (Paris: FAC, 1983); R. Laurentin, *Comment réconcilier l'exégèse et la foi* (Paris: O.E.I.L., 1984); P. Grech, *Ermeneutica e teologia biblica* (Rome: Borla, 1986); P. Grelot, *Evangiles et histoire* (Paris: Desclée, 1985). The *Theologische Quartalschrift* (Tübingen) devoted the first issue of 1979 (1-71) to the discussion of this question in the form of a symposium on J. Blank, "Exegese als theologische Basiswissenschaft" (2-23). Unfortunately, Blank's article is not very helpful, since it seems to trace the problems that have arisen around exegesis back exclusively to a dogmatism that has not yet progressed to the level of historical consciousness.

this maneuver insofar as it breaks the Bible up into discrete individual bits, which can now be applied in a new way and put to a different use in a new montage.[6] Depth-psychological "interpretations" of Scripture are only apparently more serious. Such interpretations trace the events narrated in the Bible back to mythical archetypes that supposedly emerge out of the depths of the soul and take varying forms in religious history. These archetypes are then meant to guide us on the path to the redemptive journey to healing in the ground of the soul.[7] This is but another example of reading the Scripture against its own intention. Scripture, we are now told, is not about the renunciation of the gods, but is the vehicle by which the eternal mythos of redemption is conveyed to us in the West. The fact that such forms of "interpretation" are eagerly seized on today, even worse, that they are often considered legitimate options in theology, may be the most dramatic sign of the state of emergency in which exegesis and theology find themselves.

The situation is basically the same for both Protestant and Catholic theology, although in matters of detail it can look different because of differences in scholarly tradition between the confessions. On the Catholic side, we can say that, while this situation is not the fault of the Second Vatican Council, the Council was also unable to prevent it. The Constitution on Divine Revelation attempted to hold the two sides of interpretation — historical "explanation" and holistic "understanding" — in a balanced relation. On the one hand, it emphasized the legitimacy, indeed, the necessity of the historical method, which it analyzed into three basic elements: attention to literary genres; inquiry into the historical (cultural, religious, etc.) environs; and the investigation of what is usually called the *Sitz im Leben*. At the same time, however, *Dei Verbum* also insisted on the theo-

---

6. Typical examples are the new forms of feminist and materialist biblical interpretation. See, for example, K. Füssel, "Materialistische Lektüre der Bibel," in *Methoden der Evangelien-Exegese* (ThBer 13) (Zürich: Benziger Verlag, 1985), pp. 123-63.

7. The chief representative of this increasingly popular depth-psychological exegesis is E. Drewermann, *Tiefenpsychologie und Exegese* (Olten: Walter Verlag, 1985-88). See G. Lohfink and R. Pesch, *Tiefenpsychologie und keine Exegese* (Stuttgart: Katholisches Bibelwerk, 1987); also A. Görres and W. Kasper, eds., *Tiefenpsychologische Deutung des Glaubens? Anfragen an Eugen Drewermann* (Freiburg: Herder, 1988).

logical character of exegesis and enumerated the key points of the theological method of interpreting the text: the fundamental presupposition on which theological understanding of the Bible rests is the unity of Scripture; the method that corresponds to this presupposition is that of the *"analogia fidei,"* that is, the understanding of individual texts in light of the whole. The document then offers two further indications about method. Scripture is one by reason of the historical subject that traverses it, the one people of God. To read Scripture as a unity therefore means to read it from the Church as its existential locus and to regard the faith of the Church as its true hermeneutical key. This means, on the one hand, that tradition does not obstruct access to Scripture, but opens it up; on the other hand, that the Church, in its official organs, has a decisive say in scriptural interpretation.[8]

Now, this theological canon of exegetical method admittedly stands in contradiction to the basic methodological drift of modern exegesis; this canon is indeed precisely what modern exegesis set out to overcome. Modern exegesis sees things in terms of the following dilemma: either interpretation is done critically or it is done by authority, but not both at the same time. To interpret the Bible "critically" means to leave behind any authoritative tribunal that would decide over interpretation. "Tradition," for its part, need not be rejected as an aid to understanding, but it counts only insofar as its arguments measure up to the "critical" methods. "Tradition" can under no circumstances be a criterion of interpretation. On the whole, traditional exegesis is considered to be pre-scientific and naïve; historical-critical exegesis is thought to be the first proper exploration of the text. By the same logic, the unity of the Bible itself becomes an obsolete postulate. From the historian's point of view, it is said, discontinuity, and not unity, is the rule, not only for the relationship between the Old Testament and the New Testament, but even within each of the two Testaments respectively.

Looked at in terms of assumptions like these, the task that the Council lays upon exegetes appears to be self-contradictory — at once "critical" and

---

8. See in particular chapters 11 and 12 of *Dei Verbum*; in addition, see J. Gnilka, "Die biblische Exegese im Lichte des Dekrets über die göttliche Offenbarung," in *MThZ* 36 (1985): 1-19.

"dogmatic," two irreconcilable qualities for contemporary theological thought. Now, I am personally convinced that a careful reading of the *whole* text of *Dei Verbum* can identify the essential elements needed for a synthesis between historical method and theological "hermeneutics," but the coherence between them does not simply lie ready to hand.[9] This explains why the post-conciliar reception of the document has practically set aside the theological portion of its statements as a concession to the past and has understood the text exclusively as an unrestricted official approval of the historical-critical method. This move has led to the virtual disappearance of the confessional differences between Catholic and Protestant exegesis after the Council, and this can arguably be placed in the profit column of this one-sided reception of Vatican II. The negative side of what has happened consists in the fact that the gap between exegesis and dogma has become complete now among Catholics, too. Scripture has become for them so many words from the past; everyone tries to transport to the present in his own way, without being able to put too much faith in the raft he is relying on to do the job. Faith sinks to the level of a sort of philosophy of life that the individual tries to distill from the Bible as best he can. Dogma, now deprived of grounding in Scripture, no longer holds. The Bible, detached from dogma, has become a record of past events that therefore itself belongs to the past.

The Task

This situation is not everywhere equally out in the open. The methods are not always wielded with the same radicalness, and the search for corrective elements has been under way for some time now. In this sense, we are not simply stepping onto virgin territory when we endeavor to work out a better synthesis of historical and theological methods, of criticism and dogma. On the other hand, hardly anyone is likely to affirm that we are already in possession of a convincing master idea that would do justice to the

---

9. See J. Gnilka, "Die biblische Exegese," pp. 1-9; see also A. Grillmeier's commentary in *LThK*, supplementary volume 2, pp. 528-58.

irrevocable insights of the historical method, while at the same time over-coming its limitations and opening it up to an appropriate hermeneutics. The achievement of this goal still requires the work of at least another whole generation. My remarks in what follows are meant to be part of this endeavor and to indicate a few steps that promise to advance us along this path.

It requires no special proof that escape into a supposedly purely literal understanding brings us no closer to a solution, and that a positivistic in-sistence on one's fidelity to the Church would also be an insufficient an-swer. Challenging particularly audacious and questionable hypotheses is likewise inadequate. So, too, is a lukewarm position that selects from what modern exegesis currently has on offer whichever answers happen to be the most compatible with tradition. Such caution can be useful, but it does not grasp the problem by the roots and remains arbitrary if it cannot give an intelligible account of its bases. In order to arrive at a real solution, we need to go beyond argument over details and get to the root of the matter. What we need is a criticism of the criticism. We cannot develop it from the outside, however, but only from the inside, from critical thought's own potential for self-criticism: a self-critique of historical exegesis that can be expanded into a critique of historical reason that both carries on and modi-fies Kant's critiques of reason.

I do not pretend to be able to achieve such a great task alone by some sort of coup de main. But it is necessary to begin, even if all we can do at first is some initial reconnaissance in an as-yet little-explored terrain. The historical method would have to begin its self-critique by reading its find-ings diachronically and so by taking distance from the impression of quasi-scientific certainty with which it has largely been accustomed to present its interpretations. Underlying the historical-critical method, in fact, is the ef-fort to attain results in the field of history whose degree of methodological precision and thus of certainty resembles that found in the natural sci-ences. What one exegete has concluded can subsequently be called into question only by other exegetes — this is the practical rule whose validity is generally taken for granted as downright obvious. Now, precisely be-cause exegesis takes natural science as its model, the acceptance of Heisenberg's uncertainty principle in science ought to have suggested its application to the historical method as well. Heisenberg showed that the observer's perspective is an essential determinant of the outcome of an experiment, indeed, that his questioning and observation themselves enter into and modify the "course of nature."[10] This is true a fortiori when one is dealing with historical documents: interpretation can never be simply a reproduction of "how it was." The word "inter-pretation" itself furnishes a clue to the reality: every interpretation requires from the interpreter an "inter," a going into the middle, a being with. Pure objectivity is an absurd abstraction. One does not come to know by standing apart uninvolved; rather, involvement is the antecedent condition of knowing. The only question is how to get involved in such a way that, instead of your ego shouting down the voice of the others, you achieve an inner "accord" with the reality of the past, an accord that purifies your ears for the word those others have to speak.[11]

The law that Heisenberg formulated with respect to scientific experiments expresses a state of affairs that is true of the subject-object relation quite generally. The subject cannot be kept cleanly separate from particular constellations; one can only try to place the subject in the best possible disposition. When one is dealing with history, this is true to an even greater degree, as was already said, because physical processes exist in the present and are repeatable, whereas historical events belong to the past and cannot be repeated. They contain, furthermore, the inscrutable depth characteristic of the human, and for this reason are even more dependent upon the attitude of the perceiving "subject" than processes subject to natural laws. But how do we ascertain the constellations of the subject? It is precisely at this point that what I just now called the diachronic approach to the findings of exegesis should come into play. After approximately two hundred years of historical-critical work on the texts, it is no longer possible to spread them out on a single surface and

10. See W. Heisenberg, *Das Naturbild der heutigen Physik* (Hamburg: Rowohlt, 1955) [*The Physicist's Conception of Nature* (Westport, CT: Greenwood Press, 1970)], esp. pp. 15-23.

11. I am referring here to P. Stuhlmacher, *Vom Verstehen des Neuen Testaments*, pp. 222-56, where the author formulates an answer of his own to these problems in what he calls a "hermeneutics of agreement with the biblical texts."

read them side by side. It is necessary to see them perspectivally in the context of their own history. When we do this, we realize that this history is not simply an objectively given story of progress from imprecise findings to precise and objective ones. What emerges into view is that we are dealing also and above all with a history of subjective constellations, whose trajectories correspond precisely to the developments of intellectual history and reflect them in the form of interpretations of the text. In the diachronic reading of exegesis, the latter's philosophical presuppositions present themselves readily to view. Looking at things from a distance, the observer finds to his astonishment that what would seem to be rigorously scientific, purely "historical" interpretations turn out in fact to reflect the scholar's own spirit more than they do the spirit of past ages. This need not lead to skepticism, but it should lead to a self-limitation and purification of the method.

Two Examples of Self-Criticism of the Historical-Critical Method: The Methodologies of Martin Dibelius and Rudolf Bultmann

The Main Elements of the Method and Their Presuppositions

So as to avoid remaining on the abstract level of general rules, I would like to try to illustrate what I have been saying with an actual example. In doing so, I will be relying on the dissertation written by Reiner Blank for the University of Basel entitled "Analysis and Critique of the Form-Critical Writings of Martin Dibelius and Rudolf Bultmann."[12] This book is in my judgment an outstanding example of the self-critique of the historical-critical method that I have been discussing: an exegesis that has become self-critical in the way that I mean no longer lines up "finding" after finding, no longer propounds and contests hypotheses. It looks back on its trajectory in order to recognize its foundations and to purify itself through re-

12. R. Blank, *Analyse und Kritik von Martin Dibelius und Rudolf Bultmann* (ThDiss 16) (Basel: Friedrich Reinhardt Kommissionsverlag, 1981).

flection on them. It does not thereby commit suicide. On the contrary: by limiting itself, it also identifies its proper place. Of course, the form-critical work of Dibelius and Bultmann has since their time been superseded in many respects and corrected in matters of detail. Nevertheless, their basic methodological approaches continue even today to shape the method and the ongoing story of modern exegesis. Their essential positions largely continue to underlie its historical and theological judgments. Indeed, they have to a great extent attained a kind of dogmatic status.

Both Dibelius and Bultmann were concerned to overcome the arbitrariness into which the previous phase of critical exegesis — so-called liberal theology — had fallen in its judgments about what was "historical" and what was not. The two scholars therefore went in search of rigorously literary criteria that were supposed to clarify reliably the genesis of the texts of the New Testament and thereby yield a faithful picture of the textual tradition. For this reason, Dibelius and Bultmann sought the "pure form" and the laws leading from the initial forms to the texts as we have them today. In pursuing this quest, Dibelius simply took it for granted that the way to uncover the mystery of history is to clarify how it came about.[13] But how are we supposed to get at the beginning that this theory postulates and to the laws governing the subsequent development from it? Despite all the differences between Dibelius and Bultmann in matters of detail, one can detect here a whole series of fundamental assumptions they hold in common and that both unquestioningly regard as trustworthy. Both of them assume the primacy of preaching over event: in the beginning was the word. Everything else unfolds out of preaching. Bultmann pushes this thesis to the point that only the word can be original for him; the word generates the scene.[14] Everything that is an event is accordingly by definition secondary, a clothing of the word in mythical form.

This immediately entails a further axiom that has played a constitutive role in modern exegesis ever since Dibelius and Bultmann: the idea that there is discontinuity, not only between pre-Paschal and post-Paschal tradi-

13. See R. Blank, *Analyse und Kritik*, p. 72. Critiquing this position, Kästner writes of the "superstition . . . that everything can be understood in terms of its origins": *Die Stundentrommel*, p. 120.

14. See R. Blank, *Analyse und Kritik*, p. 97.

tion, between the pre-Paschal Jesus and the nascent Church, but in every phase of the tradition as well — to the point that R. Blank could state that "Bultmann aimed at disconnection at any price."[15] One advantage of this thesis was that it proposed a way to defuse the problem of the relationship between the Old Testament and the New Testament. For if constant discontinuity is the rule already within the New Testament tradition, then its discontinuity with respect to the Old Testament no longer poses any real problem. For, on this assumption, the continuity between the two Testaments that is asserted in the New Testament writings is precisely one of those elements of mystification that the historian has unmasked as a strategy of the later community to construct a legitimacy for itself. At the same time, however, it becomes clear as if in a sudden flash just how far this retrieval of the putative origin really is from what the New Testament actually says. After all, a constitutive feature of the New Testament is the awareness of its unity with the entire witness of the Old Testament, which only now, it claims, can be understood as a unity and as a meaningful totality. The fact of the matter is that every interpretation of the New Testament has to submit to measurement by the criterion of its ability to harmonize with this fundamental conviction. Whenever this conviction is lacking, a form of understanding that recovers the intrinsic logic of the New Testament writings is excluded from the outset as a matter of principle.

Let us return to Dibelius and Bultmann. Their thesis that the simple word alone is original and that the individual phases of its development are discontinuous is connected with the opinion that only the simple can pertain to the beginning, while the complex necessarily comes later. The result is an easy-to-use parameter for the ascertainment of phases of development: the more theologically reflected and demanding a statement is, the more recent it is, and the simpler something is, the more it can be assigned to the origin.[16] But the criterion according to which we regard

15. R. Blank, *Analyse und Kritik*, p. 154.

16. See R. Blank, *Analyse und Kritik*, pp. 89-183. The practically universal assumption of this criterion is typified — to cite just one example — by the unreflecting ease with which L. Oberlinner assumes that he can apply as a criterion for dating the "reflection on matters like ecclesiology and eschatology that is doubtless more advanced (say, than Paul)" that he sees as a datum of the synoptic gospels (in his review of J. Carmignac, *La naissance*

something as more or less developed is by no means so obvious as it first appears. The judgment on that score depends essentially on the exegete's own assessments; a great deal of room is left here for arbitrariness. Above all, however, we need to challenge the idea underlying this position, which depends upon a simplistic transposition of the scientific model of evolution to the history of the spirit. Events in the spiritual order do not obey the law governing genealogies in the animal kingdom. Here the exact opposite is frequently the case: a great breakthrough is followed by generations of epigones, who reduce the audacious new beginning to the banal theories of the school, who bury it and cover it over, until, after many twists and turns, it achieves a new influence. Examples readily show the questionableness of Bultmann's and Dibelius's supposed criterion: Who would claim that Clement of Rome is more "developed" and more "complicated" than Paul? That James is more advanced than the Epistle to the Romans? That the *Didache* represents a further stage to the Pastoral Letters? Let us look at later ages: whole generations of disciples of St. Thomas were unable to grasp the greatness of his ideas; Lutheran orthodoxy is much more "medieval" than Luther himself. And even between great men this sort of evolutionary model does not hold water. Gregory the Great, for example, writes long after Augustine, with whom he is familiar, but he has translated everything from Augustine's bold vision into the simplicity of the believer's understanding. Another example: By what measure would anyone presume to declare whether Pascal is to be classified as a pre- or a post-Cartesian or which of the two thinkers is to be considered more developed? Examples could be presented from every period of history. All judgments that rest upon the theory of the discontinuity of traditions and on the evolutionistic assertion of the primacy of the "simple" over the "complicated" must therefore be called into question as being unfounded already in their basic approach.

Our task now, however, is to explain more concretely the criteria ac-

---

des Evangiles Synoptiques [Paris, 1984], in *ThRev* 83 [1987]: 194). By what criterion is one reflection to be characterized as more advanced and another as less so? That must certainly depend on the standpoint of the observer. And even if the criterion should be correct, who is to prove that an earlier or later phase follows necessarily from it?

cording to which the attempt was made to identify the "simple." In this regard there are standards as to form and content. Formally speaking, the
idea was to look for original forms. Dibelius found them in the "paradigm."
By this he meant the orally recounted model story that could supposedly
be reconstructed as the source behind the preaching. By contrast, he called
later forms the "story," the "legend," collections of narrative material, the
myth.[17] Bultmann sees the pure form in what he calls the apothegm: "The
original single piece, he claimed, is rounded and concise; at the center of interest are the words of Jesus placed at the end of the given scene; details
concerning the situation were supposedly alien to this form; Jesus,
Bultmann thought, never appears as the initiator. . . . Everything that did
not fit into this form Bultmann ascribed to later development."[18] The arbitrariness of these stipulations, which still shape theories of textual development and judgments about textual authenticity, is blatantly obvious. In
fairness, one must admit that they are not so arbitrary as may appear on
first hearing. The delimitation of the "pure form" rests after all on
Bultmann's substantive conception of the initial reality, which we must
now examine.

We have already encountered a first element of this substantive account: the thesis that the word has priority over the event. This thesis im-
plies two further pairs of antitheses: the playing off of word against cult
and of eschatology against apocalypse. Closely connected with this is the
tendency to oppose the Jewish to the Hellenistic. Among the things that
Bultmann considered Hellenistic were, for example, the idea of the cosmos, mystical religiosity, and cultic piety. The consequence is simple:
what is Hellenistic cannot be Palestinian, which is to say, it cannot be
original. What has to do with cult, cosmos, and "mysticism" has to be
ruled out as a later development. The rejection of "apocalyptic," supposedly antithetical to "eschatology," leads to yet another element: the assertion of an antagonism of the prophetic against the "legal," and so once
again against the cultic and the cosmic. A further implication of this is the
view that "ethics" is irreconcilable with the eschatological and prophetic.

17. R. Blank, *Analyse und Kritik*, pp. 11-46.
18. R. Blank, *Analyse und Kritik*, p. 98.

At the origin, we are told, is not "ethics," but an "ethos."[19] Basic decisions of Luther are surely also at work here: the dialectic of law and gospel, which makes it plausible to relegate ethics and cult to the domain of the law and so to oppose it dialectically to Jesus, who, as the bringer of the gospel, fulfills the line of the promise and thus overcomes the law. In order to understand modern exegesis and to judge it correctly, therefore, it would be necessary to reflect anew on Luther's view of the relationship between the two Testaments. For Luther replaced the analogical model that had been accepted until his day with a dialectical structure. Perhaps we could even say that Luther's shift is the real gulf separating ancient from modern exegesis.

Be that as it may, however, Luther still managed to hold all of these elements in a very subtle balance; even for Jesus himself, and thus for Christian life, both sides of the dialectic remained essential — Jesus is not only pure justification by grace, but also an "example," so that his figure also includes the ethical. When we come to Bultmann and Dibelius, however, what Luther regarded as a whole degenerates into a model of development, whose simplicity, while untenable, helps explain the model's success. Their assumed scheme fixes the picture of Jesus *a priori*. Jesus must accordingly be conceived of as strictly "Jewish." Everything "Hellenistic" has to be removed from him. Apocalyptic, sacramental, and mystical elements are ruled out of court. All that remains is a strictly "eschatological" prophet who at bottom proclaims no substantive message, but merely calls "eschatologically" to vigilance for the Wholly Other, for transcendence, which he presents to men in the form of an imminent expectation of the end of the world. This view of things gave rise to two tasks for exegesis. First, exegesis had to explain the transition from the unmessianic, unapocalyptic, unprophetic Jesus to the apocalyptic community that revered him as the Messiah; to a community in which, according to Bultmann's account of primitive Christianity, Jewish eschatology, stoic philosophy, and mystery religion supposedly became wedded in a syncre-

19. M. Dibelius, "Die Unbedingtheit des Evangeliums und die Bedingtheit der Ethik," in *ChW* 40 (1926): 1103-20, esp. 1107 and 1109; idem, *Geschichtliche und Übergeschichtliche Religion im Christentum* (Göttingen: Vandenhoeck & Ruprecht, 1925); see also R. Blank, *Analyse und Kritik*, pp. 66-71.

tistic phenomenon.[20] The second task consists in relating Jesus' original message to Christian existence today, hence, in enabling "understanding" of his call.

In principle, the model of development made this task relatively easy to achieve, although this required the mobilization of a high degree of scholarship when it came to the details. The factor responsible for producing the content of the New Testament is not seen as located in persons, but in the collective, in the "community." Romantic ideas concerning the "folk" and how it gives shape to traditions play a great role here.[21] The Hellenization thesis and the appeal to the school of *Religionsgeschichte* also exercised an influence. The work of Gunkel and Bousset came to have a decisive importance in this context.[22] The second task was more difficult. Bultmann proposed the thesis of demythologization as a way of tackling it. This thesis did not, however, yield anything like the success his theories concerning form and development put within his reach. If we may characterize somewhat crudely Bultmann's method of appropriating Jesus' message for the present, we could say that he sets up a correspondence between non-apocalyptic prophetism and certain fundamental ideas of the early Heidegger. To be a Christian according to the mind of Jesus was therefore substantially the same as the way of existing in openness and vigilance that we find depicted in Heidegger. At this point, the question inevitably arose: Was there not some simpler way of arriving at these general and largely purely formal claims?[23]

What interests us here, however, is not Bultmann the systematician, whose influence the rising tide of Marxism brought in any case to an abrupt end. Our concern here is with Bultmann the exegete, who in turn stands for a basic methodological consensus that is still quite influential in scientific

20. See R. Bultmann, *Primitive Christianity in Its Contemporary Setting* (London/New York: Thames & Hudson, 1956), esp. pp. 175ff.; see also R. Blank, *Analyse und Kritik*, pp. 172ff.

21. R. Blank, *Analyse und Kritik*, pp. 111, 175.

22. See W. Klatt, *Hermann Gunkel — Zu seiner Theologie der Religionsgeschichte und zur Entstehung der formgeschichtlichen Methode* (Göttingen: Vandenhoeck & Ruprecht, 1969).

23. See the questions that were posed in the context of the debate about demythologization. The most important contributions to this discussion are collected in the five volumes edited by H. W. Bartsch under the title *Kerygma und Mythos* (Hamburg: H. Reich, 1948-1955).

exegesis. What has emerged from our analysis is that even Bultmann the exegete is a systematician, and that his exegetical findings are not the product
of historical observation, but stem from a tissue of systematic *a priori* options. Karl Barth is correct when he writes: "Bultmann is an exegete. But I
do not think that one can dispute with him in exegetical terms, because he is
at the same time systematician, and given the kind of systematician that he
is, he would probably never deal with any given text without immediately
bringing to play certain axioms of his thought. And absolutely everything
he says stands or falls with the validity of these axioms."[24]

The Philosophical Origin of the Method

At this point the following question arises: Why did Dibelius and
Bultmann think that their essential categories of judgment — pure form,
the antithesis between the Semitic and the Greek, between the cultic and
the prophetic, between the apocalyptic and the eschatological, and so forth
— were so obviously the instruments of historical knowledge *tout court?*
Why is this system of categories, for the most part, still presupposed and
applied without question today? Since the time of Dibelius and Bultmann,
the bulk of this system has simply become one of the certainties of the
scholarship, which precedes the individual and seems legitimate because
everyone takes its application for granted. But how do things stand with
the founders of the method?

To be sure, Dibelius and Bultmann were themselves already part of a
tradition; their dependence on Gunkel and Bousset has already been mentioned. But what sort of thinking governed them as part of this tradition?
This question signals the transition from the self-criticism of the historical
method to the self-criticism of historical reason that we need in order to
keep our analysis from stopping on the surface of the issue. In the first
place, we can say that the *Religionsgeschichte* school applied the model of
evolution to the analysis of the biblical texts. It attempted, in other words,

---

24. K. Barth, *Kirchliche Dogmatik*, III, 2 (Zürich: Evangelischer Verlag, [2]1959), p. 534;
cited in R. Blank, *Analyse und Kritik*, p. 148.

to give the methods and models of natural science an application in the domain of history as well. Bultmann took this idea in a more general sense, insofar as he attributed a kind of dogmatic character to the so-called scientific worldview. He therefore took it for granted, for example, that miracles were unhistorical; the only remaining issue was to explain how the miracle narratives arose. On the one hand, the idea of the scientific world picture was vague and never thought out; on the other hand, it furnished an absolute criterion for determining what could actually have happened and what merely needed to be explained genetically. The latter category included everything that does not occur in the experience of the average man of today.[25] The only thing that can happen is what always happens, so that it was necessary to invent historical processes to account for everything else, processes whose reconstruction became the proper task of exegesis.

In my opinion, however, we must go a step deeper in order to understand the basic systematic option that generated the individual categories of judgment that Dibelius and Bultmann relied on. The real philosophical presupposition behind the whole enterprise seems to me to lie in the Kantian turn. According to Kant, man cannot perceive the voice of being in itself; he can hear it only indirectly, in the postulates of practical reason, which remain so to say as the last narrow slit through which contact with the really real, with his eternal destiny, can still reach him. For the rest, for what the activity of his reason can substantively grasp, man can go only so far as the categorial allows. He is therefore limited to the positive, to the empirical, to "exact" science, in which by definition something or someone Wholly Other, a new beginning from another plane, has no room to occur. Translated into the language of theology, this means that Revelation must retreat into the pure formality of the "eschatological" attitude, which corre-

---

25. Brilliant analyses of this can be found in P. L. Berger, *A Rumor of Angels: Modern Society and the Rediscovery of the Supernatural* (Garden City, NY: Doubleday, 1969). Just one citation here: "The present, however, remains strangely immune from relativization. In other words, the New Testament writers are seen as afflicted with a false consciousness rooted in their time, but the contemporary analyst takes the consciousness of *his* time as an unmixed intellectual blessing. The electricity and radio users are placed intellectually above the Apostle Paul" (p. 41). On the question of worldview, see the important reflections in H. Gese, *Zur biblischen Theologie* (München: Kaiser Verlag, 1977), pp. 202-22.

sponds to the tiny chink left open by Kant.[26] Everything else must be "explained": what otherwise may have appeared to be a direct disclosure of the divine can only be a myth governed by ascertainable laws of development. It is in terms of this basic conviction that Bultmann — and with him the large majority of modern exegesis — then reads the Bible. This exegesis is convinced that the events recounted in the Bible cannot really have happened as the Bible recounts them, and elaborates methods for uncovering how these events must really have happened. In this sense, modern exegesis presents a *reductio historiae in philosophiam*, a reduction of history to and by philosophy.

The real question here is thus as follows: Is it possible to read the Bible in another way? Or, putting it more correctly: Do we have to give our assent to the philosophy that constrains us to adopt such a reading? The debate about modern exegesis is not at its core a debate among historians, but among philosophers. Only on these terms can it be conducted properly; otherwise, we have nothing but swordplay in the fog. The exegetical problem is thus identical with the contemporary dispute over foundations *tout court*. A dispute of this magnitude cannot be carried on *en passant*, nor cannot it be brought to its successful issue with a few passing remarks. It requires, as was already said, the attentive, critical engagement of a whole generation. It also cannot withdraw to the Middle Ages or the Fathers and use them as a shield against the spirit of modernity. That said, it also cannot take the opposite tack of dispensing with the insights of the great believers of all ages and of acting as if the history of thought begins in earnest only with Kant. In my judgment, the recent discussion surrounding the problem of biblical hermeneutics suffers to a large extent from this restricted horizon. One does not dispose of patristic exegesis simply by labeling it "allegorical," nor can one set aside the philosophy of the Middle Ages by classifying it as "pre-critical."

---

26. See R. Blank, *Analyse und Kritik*, p. 137: "that the miracle narratives were unhistorical he [Bultmann] simply took for granted." On the Kantian philosophical background to this critique, see J. Zöhrer, *Der Glaube an die Freiheit und der historische Jesus. Eine Untersuchung der Philosophie Karl Jaspers' unter christologischem Aspekt* (Frankfurt: Peter Lang, 1986).

Basic Elements of a New Synthesis

After the foregoing remarks on the self-critical task of the historical method, we find ourselves before the positive task of using its tools in conjunction with a better philosophy that contains fewer *a prioris* foreign to the text, is less arbitrary, and offers more resources for a real listening to the text. This positive undertaking is doubtless even more difficult than the critical one. In concluding my reflections, I propose merely to cut a few initial openings in the thicket in order, I hope, to suggest where and how forward-leading paths may be found.

1. In the then contemporary dispute about theological method, Gregory of Nyssa challenged the theological rationalist Eunomius not to confuse theology with physiology (*theologein* is not *physiologein*).[27] "The mystery of theology is one thing, the science of natures is another," Gregory tells us. Now, one cannot "enclose the incomprehensible nature of God as it were in the palm of a child's hand." Gregory is alluding here to a famous remark of Zeno: "the open hand is perception, the closing hand the consent of the mind, the hand closed over the object the act of grasping it in judgment, the one hand enclosed by the other systematic science."[28] To be sure, modern exegesis, as we have seen, has relegated God to the realm of the totally ungraspable, unworldly, and so ineffable. It has done so, however, in order to be able to use the methods of natural science on the Bible itself as if it were a completely worldly thing. It practices *physiologein* on the text; it claims to be a "critical" science possessing an exactness and a certainty similar to that of natural science. This claim is false, because it rests upon a failure to recognize the dynamism and depth of the Word. It is

27. Gregory of Nyssa, *Contra Eunomium*, 10, ed. W. Jaeger, II, 3, p. 227, 26 (PG 45, 828 C); see also *Homily 11 in Cantica canticorum*: PG 44, 1013 C. We find a very similar formulation in E. Kästner, *Die Stundentrommel*, p. 117: ". . . everyone feels it to be so: science, research findings, fade into insignificance in comparison to what those wood-carvers invented in ignorance. The gain is fraudulent and paltry. The organ with which the wood-carvers sought was the more noble of the two: an eye. Historical research is only an organ for grasping. To grasp: that is, by its own testimony, its aim."

28. The formulation is from H. U. von Balthasar's introduction to *Gregor von Nyssa: Der versiegelte Quell. Auslegung des Hohen Liedes* (Einsiedeln: Johannes Verlag, ³1984), p. 17.

only by robbing it of its proper character as Word, only by violently forcing it to lie on the Procrustean bed of a few basic hypotheses, that we can subject it to such exact rules. Romano Guardini has spoken in this connection of the false security of modern exegesis, "which has produced the most significant individual findings, but has lost its proper object, and so has ceased to be theology at all."[29] Another magnificent passage of Gregory of Nyssa, in which he affirms just the opposite, points us in the right direction: "Those tremulous and twinkling lights of the divine words that spread their gleam over the eyes of the soul are stars. . . . But if what we hear of Elijah should happen to our soul as well, if our thought would be snatched up in a fiery chariot . . . then we would not need to give up hope of approaching those stars, by which I mean the divine thoughts."[30] My point in citing this passage is not to plead for some sort of enthusiasm; the point is rather that there is no getting around the demand for readiness to open oneself to the dynamism of the Word. For the Word can be brought to understanding only in a sympathy that is ready to experience something new, to be taken on a new path. What is required is not the closed hand, but the open eye. . . .

2. Accordingly, the exegete must also refrain from approaching the interpretation of the text with a ready-made philosophy, with the dictate of a so-called modern or "scientific" worldview, which stipulates what may exist and what may not. He must not rule out *a priori* the possibility that God can speak in his own voice in the world using human words; he must

29. R. Guardini, *Das Christusbild*, p. 14. The reflections on method that Guardini develops on pages 7-15 of this work are, in my opinion, among the most important things that have ever been said on the problem of methodology in scriptural interpretation. Guardini deals extensively with this problem already in his early period in his essay "Heilige Schrift und Glaubenswissenschaft," in *Die Schildgenossen* 8 (1928): 24-57 (Italian version: "Sacra Scrittura e scienza della fede," in I. de la Potterie, R. Guardini, J. Ratzinger, G. Colombo, and E. Bianchi, *L'esegesi cristiana oggi* [Piemme: Casale Monferrato ³2000], pp. 45-91). M. Theobald critically engages with Guardini's theory and practice of exegesis in "Die Autonomie der historischen Kritik — Ausdruck des Unglaubens oder theologische Notwendigkeit? Zur Schriftauslegung R. Guardini's," in L. Honnefelder and M. Lutz-Bachmann, eds., *Auslegungen des Glaubens. Zur Hermeneutik christlicher Existenz* (Berlin/Hildesheim: Morus Verlag, 1987), pp. 21-45.

30. Gregory of Nyssa, *Homily 10 in Cantica canticorum*: PG 44, 980 B-C.

not rule out the possibility that God can work in history and enter into it without ceasing to be himself, however improbable this might appear. He must be ready to take instruction from the phenomenon. He must be ready to accept that one of the things that can happen in history is a real beginning, which as such cannot be derived from any prior given, but opens itself from out of itself.[31] He must also avoid denying man's possession of a capacity to listen extending beyond the categories of pure reason, to transcend himself into the open and infinite truth of being.

We should add that the problem that concerns us here, though penetratingly formulated by Kant, was certainly seen by the Fathers and the great theologians of the Middle Ages. Gregory of Nyssa, for example, writes in one passage that "the creature as a whole is not capable of placing itself . . . outside of itself. It remains always in itself. Whatever it may be able to perceive, it perceives itself."[32] In the same vein, Thomas Aquinas says that human knowing does not attain the truth in itself, but always reaches a human reality, which, however, does lead to the discovery of other truths. Put in other terms, truths of the spiritual order are always grasped only metaphorically, by means of other things.[33] That said, the great theologians characteristically refuse to make this, for them, evident philosophical claim the criterion of what can be true in the biblical accounts. Rather, they let their thinking be enlarged by the phenomenon of the biblical Word as it encounters them. Gregory of Nyssa does this in two ways. Man finds himself imprisoned in the jail of his creaturely being and knowing, but he carries in himself a yearning for escape, an arrow pointing him in the direction of infinite love. And that is precisely where God shows himself as he is in himself. Man is a mirror of God himself, and when man perceives himself as a whole, he perceives more than himself: he perceives the mirroring of the pure light within himself. Man cannot get beyond himself, but God can get into him. In the dyna-

---

31. R. Guardini, *Das Christusbild*, p. 11.

32. H. U. von Balthasar, *Gregor von Nyssa: Der versiegelte Quell*, 16; idem, *Présence et pensée. Essai sur la philosophie religieuse de Grégoire de Nysse* (Paris: Beauchesne, 1942).

33. *Summa Theologiae*, I, q. 88, art. 1 c; see also q. 84, art. 7; 13, 6. See in addition the important work of M. Arias-Reyero, *Thomas von Aquin als Exeget* (Einsiedeln: Johannes Verlag, 1971), pp. 176 and 204, on which I rely in what follows.

mism of his being, man can also transcend himself; he becomes more like God, and likeness is knowing — we know what we are, no more and no less. This first idea is paired with a second one in Gregory: God's entrance into man has taken historical form in the Incarnation. The individual human monads are broken open into the new subject that is the new Adam. God wounds the soul — the Son is this wound, and by this wound we are opened up. The new subject, the Adam who finds his unity in the Church, opens from within to be in contact with the Son, and so with the triune God himself.[34] Thomas Aquinas gave these two ideas a metaphysical turn in the principles of analogy and participation. By doing so, he made possible an open philosophy that is capable of accepting the biblical phenomenon in all its radicalism. Instead of the dogmatism of a supposedly scientific world picture, the challenge for today would be to think further in the direction of this kind of open philosophy, in order to recover the presuppositions necessary for an understanding of the Bible.[35]

3. By the same token, the relationship between event and word must also be newly appraised. For Dibelius, Bultmann, and the mainstream of modern exegesis, the event represents irrationality; it belongs to the domain of pure facticity, which is composed of chance and necessity. For this reason, fact as such cannot be the bearer of meaning. The meaning lies only in the word, and whenever events seem to be themselves bearers of meaning, they have to be considered as illustrations of the word, and must be reducible to it. Admittedly, judgments flowing from this intellectual approach have a high degree of evidence for contemporary man. This evidence reflects today's regnant plausibility structure, but it does not at all follow that it is based on the structure of reality as such. Evidence of this sort is valid only on the assumption that the methodological principle of natural science, which holds that everything that occurs is susceptible of a causal explanation in terms of purely immanent efficiencies, is not only a methodological hypothesis, but is true in itself. On this assumption, there

---

34. H. U. von Balthasar, *Gregor von Nyssa: Der versiegelte Quell*, pp. 10-24.

35. Rich material for this task can be found in M. Arias-Reyero, *Thomas von Aquin*, especially on pages 192-206.

is indeed only "chance and necessity," nothing more, and it is legitimate to regard facts as *bruta facta*. But what is useful as a methodological principle of natural science is already a banality as a philosophical principle; as a theological one, it is absurd. If for no other reason than to satisfy scientific curiosity, we need to experiment here with precisely the opposite principle: that things can also be different.

Once again, Thomas Aquinas, who recapitulates the philosophical thinking of more than one and a half millennia, can serve as an indication of a counter-model. Thomas holds that nature, the heavenly bodies, things in general, life, and time all follow a certain course, that is, a movement directed towards a goal. When things have reached their goal, one can discover the true sense that so to say lay hidden in them. This sense appearing at the end of the movement transcends whatever sense might be inferred from any given section of the now completed path. "This new sense thus presupposes the existence of a divine Providence, the existence of a (salvation) history arriving at its destination."[36] God's action thus appears as the principle of the intelligibility of history. The unifying principle of the whole of past and present "history, which alone confers sense on it, is, however, the historical event of Christ. This event also gives the future its unity."[37] "The epochs of human history are united by a deed"[38] — by the deed of Christ; it is on this deed that man's relation to God rests. "The whole of history and the whole of Scripture must be looked at in terms of this deed."[39] This means, then, that the deeds that occurred in the Old Testament have their basis in a future deed in light of which it first becomes possible to understand them correctly. This means, in turn, that word, reality, and history are not separate from one another. "For the Word of God works what it signifies; it allows for no separation between deed and word."[40]

Put another way, the event itself can be a "word," a fact reflected by the

36. M. Arias-Reyero, *Thomas von Aquin*, p. 85. Arias provides ample textual evidence from the writings of Thomas.

37. M. Arias-Reyero, *Thomas von Aquin*, p. 106.

38. M. Arias-Reyero, *Thomas von Aquin*, p. 107.

39. M. Arias-Reyero, *Thomas von Aquin*, p. 107.

40. M. Arias-Reyero, *Thomas von Aquin*, p. 102.

biblical terminology.[41] Two important fundamental rules for interpretation follow from this:

a. If we wish to remain within the specific perspective of the Bible, we need to consider word and event as equi-primordial. The dualism between word and event, which banishes the event into the realm of the word-less, which is to say, into the realm of the sense-less, actually robs the word itself of its capacity to mediate sense, because the word then stands in a world from which all sense has been stripped. It leads to a docetic Christology, in which the reality, that is, the concrete bodily existence of Christ and of men in general, is removed from the domain of sense. But when this happens, the essence of the biblical witness is missed.

b. Now, such a dualism also cuts the biblical Word off from creation and undoes the coherence of sense between the Old and New Testaments in favor of a principle of discontinuity. When the intimate connection between word and event is no longer retained, there is also no longer any unity of Scripture. A New Testament separated from the Old, however, cannot hold together even on its own terms, because, according to its own claim, it exists only thanks to this unity. The principle of discontinuity must therefore yield to the principle of the *analogia Scripturae* that emerges from the intrinsic claim of the biblical text itself; the principle of mechanism must give way to a principle of teleology.[42] True, texts must first be restored to their historical locus and interpreted in their historical context. But this must be followed by a second phase of interpretation, however, in which they must also be seen in light of the entire historical movement and in terms of the central event of Christ. There is no understanding of the Bible until both methods operate in harmony. If the first phase of interpretation was largely absent from the Fathers and the Middle Ages, so that the second phase easily lapsed into caprice, it is this second phase that we are lacking today. The result is that the first phase becomes trivial, indeed; the

41. Cf. also J. Bergmann, H. Lutzmann, and W. H. Schmidt, *"dabar,"* in *TDOT* II, pp. 84-125; O. Procksch, *"legō ktl,"* in *TDNT* 4, pp. 91-100. On the unity of word and event in Thomas, cf. M. Arias-Reyero, *Thomas von Aquin,* pp. 102 and 246.

42. For a correct understanding of teleology, see R. Spaemann and R. Löw, *Die Frage Wozu? Geschichte und Wiederentdeckung des teleologischen Denkens* (München/Zürich: Piper, 1981).

denial of coherent sense leads here, too, to methodological arbitrariness. To discover how each given historical word intrinsically transcends itself, and thus to recognize the intrinsic rightness of the rereadings by which the Bible progressively interweaves event and sense, is one of the tasks of objective interpretation. It is a task for which suitable methods can and must be found. In this sense, the exegetical maxim of Thomas Aquinas is very much to the point: "The task of the good interpreter is not to consider words, but sense."[43]

4. In order to give an account of, and to make methodologically accessible, how the individual texts of Scripture transcend themselves into the whole, the tradition has formulated a second principle in addition to the first (which consisted in taking Christ as the center of the Bible): the "Christological" view is complemented by a properly "theological" one in the strict sense of the word.[44] This means that all the words of Scripture are human words and are initially to be interpreted as such. But they rest upon "revelation," that is, on the fact of being touched by an experience that transcends the store of experience possessed by the author himself. God is speaking in human words, and this gives rise to the peculiar incongruence of the concrete word vis-à-vis its origin. In today's theological lingo, it is common to term the Bible "Revelation" without qualification. This usage would never have occurred to the ancients. Revelation is a dynamic event between God and man, which again and again becomes reality only in their encounter. The biblical Word attests to Revelation, but does not contain it in the sense of absorbing it and turning it into a sort of thing that one could stick in one's pocket. The Bible attests to Revelation, but the concept of Revelation as such is broader. Practically, this means that a text can say more than its author himself was capable of conceiving at the moment of writing it.[45]

---

43. "*Officium est enim boni interpretis non considerare verba, sed sensum*": *In Matthaeum*, XXVII, I, n. 2321; ed. R. Cai (Torino/Roma: Marietti, 1951), p. 358; cf. M. Arias-Reyero, *Thomas von Aquin*, p. 161.

44. M. Arias-Reyero, *Thomas von Aquin*, pp. 153-262.

45. I take the liberty of referring to my analysis of the concept of Revelation in the works of Bonaventure: J. Ratzinger, *The Theology of History in St. Bonaventure* (Chicago: Franciscan Herald Press, 1971), especially pp. 56-59; a few remarks can also be found in my lecture "Buchstabe und Geist des Zweiten Vatikanums in den Konzilsreden von Kardinal

This is true already of great literary texts; it is especially true of the biblical Word. The sense of the individual text exceeds its immediate historical standpoint. For this reason, it is also possible to revisit the text in a new historical setting and to place it within new webs of meaning — the justification of *relecture*. By the same token, the totality of Scripture occupies a level of its own; it is more than a tapestry pieced together from what the individual authors could have intended in their given historical emplacement. One does not yet have the whole by having all of the parts individually. What Martin Buber once said about his collaboration with Franz Rosenzweig on their translation of the Bible should therefore be true of all exegesis. They were of course very attentive to the various strata of source material discovered in our day, and they labeled them with the usual abbreviations. Their aim, however, was not to translate individual voices. Rather, their ultimate criterion was the concrete wholeness of the biblical text, which they designated with the abbreviation R. On the level of technical exegesis, this sign meant simply "Redactor." But amongst themselves, Buber and Rosenzweig translated it with "Rabbenu" — our teacher. The text in its wholeness is "our teacher." In its wholeness, it expresses an intention that goes beyond the conjectured intentions of the individual sources.[46] Interpretation can certainly (and perhaps must) concern itself with J, P, E, etc. Nevertheless, the ultimate goal of correct interpretation must be to understand R, that is, the actual biblical text as an intrinsically meaningful whole.

5. In the last hundred years, exegesis has achieved great things, but it has also produced great errors, errors that have also partly become academic dogmas, which many deem it virtually a sacrilege to call into question, especially when non-exegetes are doing the questioning. As great an exegete as Heinrich Schlier once warned his colleagues against wasting their time on useless matters.[47] J. Gnilka has repeated this warning in a more specific

---

Frings," in *Communio.de* 16 (1987): 251-65. See also K. Rahner and J. Ratzinger, *Offenbarung und Überlieferung* (Freiburg: Herder, 1965) [*Revelation and Tradition* (New York: Herder & Herder, 1966)], pp. 34-38.

46. M. Buber, "Zu einer neuen Verdeutschung der Schrift," in M. Buber and F. Rosenzweig, *Die Fünf Bücher der Weisung* (Köln: Jakob Hegner, 1954), pp. 7f. and 40f.

47. H. Schlier, "Was heißt Auslegung der Heiligen Schrift?" in *Besinnung auf das Neue Testament. Exegetische Aufsätze und Vorträge II* (Freiburg: Herder, 1964), p. 62.

form by criticizing an excessive emphasis on the history of textual transmission.[48] In the same vein, I would like to spell out the following *desiderata*:

a. The time for a thorough new reflection on the methodology of exegesis seems to have come. Scientific exegesis needs to recognize the philosophical element in a whole series of its basic axioms. In light of this fact, it must also test the findings that rest on these axioms.

b. Exegesis can no longer be studied in a linear-synchronic fashion, after the manner of scientific discoveries, which do not depend upon their history, but only on how exactly they measure their data. Exegesis needs to recognize its own nature as a historical discipline. Its history belongs to its being. In critically classifying its respective positions within the whole of its history, it will recognize the relativity of its judgments, on the one hand, while being better equipped to penetrate to the real, albeit always unfinished, understanding of the biblical Word, on the other.

c. Philological and literary methods are, and remain, of decisive importance for correct exegesis. But their genuinely critical application includes — precisely when we are dealing with a text that makes a claim such as the Bible does — an awareness of the philosophical implications of the interpretive process. The self-critical study of its own history on the part of exegesis must also be a study of the essential philosophical alternatives facing human thought. Nor can such a requirement be satisfied simply by looking at the last 150 years. The major proposals of patristic and medieval thought must also be taken into consideration. It is equally indispensable to reflect upon the basic decisions of the Reformation with their implications for the history of exegesis.

d. We do not need at the moment any new hypotheses about the *Sitz im Leben,* about possible sources and the processes of transmission associated with them. We need a critical reconnaissance of the exegetical landscape in order to get back to the text and to separate the promising hypotheses from the unhelpful ones. Only under these conditions, moreover, can a new, fruitful collaboration between exegesis and systematic theology emerge; only thus can exegesis truly be at the service of the understanding of the Bible.

48. J. Gnilka, "Die biblische Exegese," p. 14.

e. The exegete must realize that he does not occupy a neutral position above or outside history of the Church. This sort of fancied immediacy of access to the purely historical can only short-circuit exegesis. The first presupposition of all exegesis is that it takes the Bible as *one* book. If it does so, then it has already chosen for itself a position that is rooted in much more than the literary aspects of the text. It has recognized this literature as the product of a coherent history, and this history as the proper locus of understanding. If it wishes to be theology, it must take a further step: it must acknowledge that the faith of the Church is precisely the sort of sym-pathy without which the text remains closed. It must acknowledge this faith as the hermeneutic, as the locus of understanding, which does not dogmatically force itself upon the Bible, but is the only way of letting it be itself.

Having said this, we have returned to our starting point. The dead ends of the critical method have once again made it clear that understanding requires the understander — the key without which the text has nothing to say to the present. It remains Bultmann's great achievement that he brought out clearly the necessity of hermeneutics, even though he remained a prisoner of presuppositions that to a large extent invalidate his solutions. Perhaps the impasse of present-day efforts can serve a new understanding of the fact that the faith is truly the spirit out of which the Scripture was born and is therefore the only door that leads into its inner heart.

Translated by Adrian Walker

Biblical Exegesis: A Science of Faith

Ignace de la Potterie

On the occasion of the colloquium organized in 1986 by the École française of Rome, entitled "The Second Vatican Council (1959-1965)," I was asked to present a vast and complex theme: "Vatican II and the Bible." I accepted the invitation with some trepidation,[1] noting that it is still too early to measure with precision all the importance of the conciliar shift on this topic. So far, however, we can agree with what a well-known Italian theologian, S. Dianich, wrote a few years ago: "The heart of the Council lies in this: it reopened the issue of *interpretation in faith* . . . [and] gave new impetus to the process of the *hermeneutic demand*."[2] This is particularly true for the interpretation of Scripture. Exegetes are invited to reflect more deeply on the epistemological status of their discipline: What does it mean to "interpret Sacred Scripture" in today's cultural context, and in the situation of the Church after Vatican II? In the last few years, I have had several opportunities to grapple with this question.[3] I would like to continue my reflection in

1. Cf. the volume of the acts of the colloquium: *Le deuxième Concile du Vatican (1954-1965)* (Collection de l'École française de Rome, 113) (Rome: École française, 1989), pp. 477-96.

2. In the collective volume, *A vent'anni dal Concilio: Chiesa e società dopo il Vaticano II* (Pisa: ETS Editrice, 1985), p. 93 (italics mine).

3. I permit myself to mention some of these: "Préface" to B. de Margerie, *Introduction à l'histoire de l'exégèse*, vol. 1 (Paris: Cerf, 1980), pp. i-vii; "Préface: Exégèse, philosophie et

this article, which represents the culmination of long teaching experience, ten years in Louvain and thirty at the Biblical Institute in Rome. This is, then, a little like an academic will and testament: I will inquire, on the one hand, into the current situation of exegesis in the Church, and on the other, into the possibilities whose vistas open up before us into the years to come.

We will begin with a general assertion. Contemporary culture is permeated by a positivistic mentality that is the result of immense progress in science and technology. The generalized use of the *computer* can be taken as a symbol of this invasion of a scientific mentality. As a consequence of this invasion, the truth risks being reduced, for the *homo faber* of our age, to the scientific and material verification of objects. According to the opinion of M. Henry, we are threatened by a "technical-scientific ideology that sees scientific knowledge as the only legitimate type of knowledge, the only real thing, the only truth."[4] Another philosopher, B. Ronze, warns us of the danger facing today's "man of quantity," in which the accumulation of positive facts through scientific means invites its counterpart, the "agony of meaning."[5] The precision of "knowledge" goes hand in hand with a loss of "understanding," at least insofar as *human* realities are concerned. With regard to the latter, science remains impotent; gaining access to this sphere requires personal reflection, long experience, and wisdom, not to mention faith. These fundamental problems of our cultural situation have begun to concern the best thinkers of our time, as we saw at an international symposium held some time ago in Tokyo.[6]

---

herméneutique," in P. Toinet, *Pour une théologie de l'exégèse* (Paris: FAC-éditions, 1983), pp. 13-24; "La 'lecture dans l'Esprit': La manière patristique de lire la Bible est-elle encore possible aujourd'hui?" in *Communio.de* 11 (1986): 11-27; "La vérité de l'Écriture et l'herméneutique biblique, in *RThL* 18 (1987): 171-86; "Interpretation of the Holy Scripture in the Spirit in Which It Was Written (Dei Verbum 12c)," in R. Latourelle, ed., *Vatican II — Assessment and Perspectives*, vol. 1 (New York: Paulist Press, 1988), pp. 220-66.

4. Cf. M. Henry, *La barbarie* (Paris: B. Grasset, 1987); for the sentence quoted, cf. the presentation of the work by P. Masset, in *NRT* 109 (1987): 416-18 (p. 416).

5. B. Ronze, *L'homme de quantité* (Paris: Gallimard, 1977), pp. 101-3; cf. also pp. 64-71: "the death of explication"; pp. 105-29: "the quantification of the spirit"; we are then invited to a "dequantification" (Part II) and to a "conquest of meaning" (pp. 217-43).

6. Cf. L. Morren, "Science, technologie et valeurs spirituelles: Un symposium à Tokyo," in *NRT* 111 (1989): 83-96.

This global problem obviously has powerful repercussions on the religious sciences. The Kantian rupture (cf. *Religion within the Limits of Reason Alone*), the rupture of the Enlightenment and then of positivism, were above all ruptures between science and faith; in this way, an attempt was made to guarantee the autonomy of reason. From this flowed the growing secularization of the ecclesial sciences. In fundamental theology, the question is raised whether or not the practitioner of this discipline must be a believer. Moral theologians discuss whether they can still speak of a Christian ethics or if they ought rather to admit only a general deontology (and here, too, they remain divided: Is ethics founded on human nature or the social consensus of the majority, or the person in his existential reality?). An analogous problem surfaces in canon law: Is it merely a juridical science, like civil law, or a genuinely theological science?[7] Curiously enough, the same question has been raised in Church history: Is it only a historical discipline, or is it part of theology?[8] The same, again, for the history of patristic exegesis: Must it limit itself to positivistic and historical research?[9] As we can see, it is a global calling into question.

In the end, we arrive at our discipline, biblical exegesis. The same basic problem has existed here for some time. From the last century onward, the conviction has spread that the only really "scientific" and modern method in exegesis is the "historical-critical" method:[10] the exegesis of a book of the Bible should be only the study of its sources and of the historical environment of its author, followed by a study of the philological and literary aspects of the text. Under no circumstances ought it to venture onto the terrain of theology. But this is precisely the whole problem! Some even go so far as to affirm that one must attentively distinguish (scientific) exegesis

7. Cf. J. Gaudemet, "Théologie et droit canon," in the volume cited in the following footnote, pp. 160-66.

8. Cf. the acts of the colloquium of the Campo Santo Teutonico di Roma: *Grundfragen der Kirchengeschichtlichen Methode heute*, under the direction of K. Repgen, published in the *RQ* 80 (1985): 1-258; presentation of R. Aubert, in *RHE* 33 (1988): 839-40.

9. Cf. the acts of the annual colloquia of the new Italian association: *Annali di storia dell'esegesi* (beginning in 1984).

10. A special issue of *Concilium* (n. 158, Oct. 1980) was dedicated to this theme: *Conflicting Ways of Interpreting the Bible*.

and (theological) interpretation. The latter would no longer be rigorously scientific. So we come to the disconcerting paradox that, contrary to the entire ancient tradition, the task of the exegete would no longer be that of *interpreting* Scripture or of seeking its *sense*, but solely that of reconstructing its historical genesis and then explaining the texts from a cultural, philological, and literary point of view. The fact that exegesis is no longer interested in what the Bible means for the believer today shows in a disquieting fashion that we have fallen into a kind of "epistemological unconsciousness" (Clodovis Boff), that is, a real incapacity to scrutinize the depth dimension of the text, what Paul Ricoeur aptly calls "the life of the text." Fortunately, in our day the hermeneutic demand is surfacing everywhere; the restless search for *meaning* has happily called into question trust in the exclusive use of the historical-critical method. In his article "Biblical Interpretation in Conflict,"[11] Joseph Cardinal Ratzinger noted that nowadays, it is almost common parlance to speak of a crisis in the use of this method. But what are the alternatives?

As strange as it may seem, at bottom, this is the problem the Council implicitly wanted to address in the dogmatic constitution *Dei Verbum*. It is a little-known fact that one of the reasons that prompted the Church to come up with a Constitution on Revelation was that, after the publication of Pius XII's encyclical *Divino Afflante Spiritu* (1943), it became increasingly clear that "the application of historical and critical methods in the *interpretation* of Scripture posed a *theological* problem."[12] Because of this, the Council wished to integrate Scripture into Revelation, which was called, precisely, *Dei Verbum*; and it went so far as boldly to say that the study of Sacred Scripture must be, "as it were, the soul of sacred theology" (DV 24). Thus today, we witness the emergence of many burning questions.

---

11. Initially published in German in *Schriftauslesung im Widerstreit* (ed. J. Ratzinger) (QD 117) (Freiburg: Herder, 1989), pp. 15-44, then in English as *Biblical Interpretation in Crisis: The Ratzinger Conference on Bible and Church* (Grand Rapids: Eerdmans, 1989), pp. 1-23; also in Italian, French, and Spanish. A fresh, full English version can be read in this volume.

12. J. Ratzinger, "Dogmatische Konstitution über die göttliche Offenbarung: Einleitung," in *LThK*, Ergänzungsband II (Das zweite Vaticanische Konzil) (Freiburg: Herder, 1967), pp. 498-503 (cf. p. 499).

What is the relationship between the Bible and the *Word of God?* What is the *sense* of Scripture? What is a *Christian* interpretation of Scripture? What is the relationship between Scripture and *Tradition,* Scripture and the *Church, faith* and *science,* exegesis and *theology?*

In any case, it is important to pose the question on a rigorously epistemological level. In the methodological reflections that follow, we will take our principal inspiration from Scripture itself, then from the patristic tradition, and lastly from the conciliar Constitution *Dei Verbum.* On the philosophical plane, we will try to be attuned to instances of contemporary hermeneutics (Blondel, Ricoeur, Gadamer, Pareyson, Ladrière). On the plane of theology, we drew great profit from a study of Romano Guardini's, "Sacred Scripture and the Science of Faith";[13] though written long ago, it has sparked considerable interest in the past few years, occasioned by the centenary celebration of the birth of the author (1885-1985). For this reason, the title of the present article substantially takes up that of Guardini's.[14]

We will proceed in two steps. First, we will examine the *object* of our research, Sacred Scripture. We will reflect on the fact that, according to the entire Judeo-Christian tradition, the Bible is both a human word and the Word of God. From this, it follows for the *subject* who interprets, the exegete, that if he really wants to understand and interpret Sacred Scripture, he must necessarily employ a twofold approach to the text: the approach of science and that of faith. The interpretation of Scripture in the *complete* sense must be theological; in other words, it is a "science of faith." This will be the theme of the second part.

---

13. R. Guardini, "Heilige Schrift und Glaubenswissenschaft," in the little-known review, *Die Schildgenossen* 8 (1928): 24-57. Italian version: "Sacra Scrittura e scienza della fede," in *L'esegesi cristiana oggi,* 45-91 (see above p. 21 n. 29); an abridged French version, in R. Guardini, H. de Lubac, H. Urs von Balthasar, J. Ratzinger, and I. de la Potterie, *L'exégèse chrétienne aujourd'hui* (Paris: Fayard, 2000), pp. 19-32.

14. A good presentation of Guardini's position can be found in the work of F. Wechsler, *Romano Guardini als Kerygmatiker* (Paderborn: Schöning, 1973), pp. 174-82: "Die Schriftauslesung Guardinis" ["The Interpretation of Scripture in Guardini"]. For a more critical reaction (cf. below), see M. Theobald, "Die Autonomie der historischen Kritik — Ausdruck des Unglaubens oder theologische Notwendigkeit? Zur Schriftauslesung Guardinis," in L. Honnefelder and M. Lutz-Bachmann, eds., *Auslegung des Glaubens: Zur Hermeneutik christlicher Existenz* (Bern/Berlin/Hildesheim: Morus, 1987), pp. 21-45.

The Bible: Human Word and Word of God

With Romano Guardini, we will take as our starting point a general epistemological norm, which we will apply immediately to biblical exegesis. All its reasoning can be expressed in a syllogism: no object of research can be understood well except by a mode of knowledge adequate to its object. Thus, the knowing subject must be qualified to attain such a specific mode of knowledge; at the same time, he must be willing to make use of it in his research. Now, for us Christians, the texts of the Bible are at one and the same time the words of human authors and the instrument of the Word of God (for brevity's sake, we also say that it is the Word of God). Consequently, if someone really wants to "understand" Sacred Scripture in a manner that conforms to that which it *really is*, he must make a double effort of understanding: that demanded by any literary or historical text and that which seeks to understand Scripture as the transmission of the Word of God, or Revelation.

We begin by developing the lesser premise of this syllogism. Hence, we ask a fundamental question: What is the Bible?

The Bible as Human Word

By now, everyone, even within the Church, acknowledges the fact that the texts of the Bible were written by human authors in a particular historical and cultural situation. After the modernist crisis, the encyclical *Divino Afflante Spiritu* was the document in which the Church definitively accepted the use of the philological and historical method in the study of the Bible. Of course, the encyclical also affirms the need for an exact use of the spiritual senses of Scripture, and encourages exegetes to study the Fathers of the Church and the most renowned commentators of the past (EB 550-554). But it was not these entirely classical recommendations that drew attention. Rather, it was the much more novel fact that, according to the encyclical, the exegete's "foremost and greatest endeavor should be to discern and define clearly that sense of the biblical words which is called literal" (EB 550). To seek that which the author wanted to say is "the *supreme law* of interpretation" (EB 557). To this end, exegetes must bear in mind the particular character of the sacred writer, of the literary genres employed in his times, and all the antiquity of the biblical age that could help toward a better understanding of the author's thought (EB 555-561). Today, these norms are universally acknowledged. Knowledge of the languages, the study of the historical context, and comparison with other literature of the age are currently practiced in the interpretation of profane books of different times; these must be equally employed in the interpretation of the Bible.

This is almost too obvious. Nevertheless, where Sacred Scripture is concerned, today we see much more clearly all the hermeneutical ambiguities and theological lacunae of such a method, if it limits itself to seeking out the literal sense of the Bible. An aspect of this can be dangerously reductive: it runs the not-at-all illusory risk of seeing in the Bible merely one historical document among many others, "a book like the others" in the words of Renan; doubtless the chief witness to the religious literature of Israel and the first Christians, but not the witness to divine Revelation. Certainly, even the Constitution *Dei Verbum* says that "due attention must be paid both to the customary and characteristic styles of feeling, speaking and narrating which prevailed at the time of the sacred writer" (DV 12:2). But this affirmation is immediately followed by a truly novel paragraph on the ecclesial interpretation of Sacred Scripture "in the sacred Spirit in which it was written" (DV 12:3); strangely enough, after the Council, this remained a dead letter. On the other hand, if it is true that in order to interpret the Bible, we must pay attention to profane literature, we absolutely cannot forget this fundamental principle: even when the sacred writer makes use of modes of expression that prevailed at his time, he uses them according to a new perspective. His thought can never be reduced to that of the profane authors from whom he often drew inspiration. Even when it is materially similar or identical to its Jewish or pagan models, his text takes on a *new sense* in the *new context* of Sacred Scripture.

Let us look at two concrete cases. Today, everyone acknowledges that the prophetic theme of the covenant was elaborated according to the model and the literary form of the bilateral pacts of the ancient Near East. But the biblical Covenant is new in two ways: first, the parties entering into it are no longer two sovereign powers, but God and man. Second, the pro-visions of this covenant are of a new kind: the law will be written in men's hearts (Jer 31:31). In the New Testament, we will take as an example the word *kecharitōmenē* in the angel's greeting to Mary (Luke 1:28).[15] The only two pre-Christian uses of this verb *(charitoō)* can be found in Alexandrian Judaism, both in the same verbal form of the perfect participle. This parti-ciple designates both an "amiable" man (Sir 18:17) and a "shapely" woman (Sir 9:8, cited by Clement of Alexandria), which means that it still had a profane sense. But in a most felicitous intuition, Clement's disciple Origen guessed that in the gospel text, the meaning must be different;[16] the angel did not come to declare that Mary was "gracious" (a ridiculous interpreta-tion that we find later in Erasmus and Luther), but rather that, through the work of grace, she has been "rendered pleasing" to God. We pass beyond human grace to the grace of God. This is one of the many particularly in-teresting cases in which we can witness, almost empirically, the genesis and development of the Christian language. But in order to see this, in order to understand it, and in order to accept this transformation of language in ex-egesis, philology is no longer enough. A special sensibility is needed on the part of the reader; he needs a willingness to welcome the realities of faith. In texts like this, the desire to preserve at all costs the meaning the words had in pre-Christian models is a methodologically false historical ap-proach: the reader does not see (or does not want to see) their *new sense*. Now, this new sense is the literal sense, which, however, has become a spir-itual sense.

At this point we discover the limited value of the study of the sources. With great perspicuity, Paul Ricoeur for some time now has denounced the "illusion of the sources."[17] This is important from a hermeneutical point of view: the biblical text acquires a new meaning, different from the

---

15. Cf. my two articles: "*Kecharitōmenē* en Lc 1, 28," in *Bib* 68 (1987): 357-82; 480-508.

16. We demonstrated this in more detail in "L'annuncio a Maria: Lc 1, 28 e 1, 35b nel kerigma di Luca e nella catechesi dei Padri," in S. Felici, ed., *La Mariologia nella catechesi dei Padri (Età prenicena)* (Rome: LAS, 1989), pp. 19-34.

17. Cf. his closing address at the Congress at Chantilly, in the volume *Exégèse et herméneutique* (Paris: Éditions du Seuil, 1971), pp. 285-95 (here, p. 292). He identifies two other illusions: "the illusion of the author" and the "illusion of the intended audience."

meaning of its Jewish or pagan models. The author reinterprets these. But where does this new meaning come from? Obviously not from the historical models, since the author is distancing himself from them. It can only come from something interior, from the *faith* the author shares with the other members of the people of God — first Israel, then the Church — and which he seeks to express precisely for them. His words are the expression of his faith, but it is no less true that *his faith transforms the sense of his words.*

Thus, it is clear that even if we take as our starting point the biblical text as human word, we are already obliged to consider it under an aspect that is not merely literary and historical. Rather, we must see it as a document that expresses the faith of its author (we add: and his inspiration), that is, an attitude of openness and welcome in the face of revelation.

The Bible and the Word of God

For one of the last things he wrote, a commentary on the Sunday readings, Hans Urs von Balthasar chose the title "God Speaks to Us in Scripture." This is of course a traditional formula, but it remains surprising: in the texts of the Bible, which were written by *men* long ago, it is *God* himself who speaks. And it is not addressed merely to the men of biblical times, but to all of us *today.* This brief phrase of Balthasar's encapsulates the profound conviction of the entire Tradition. We recall, for example, a famous text of St. Gregory the Great, who was inspired in turn by St. Augustine: "What is Sacred Scripture if not a letter from God Omnipotent to his creature? . . . So dedicate yourself to study, I beg you, and meditate each day on the words of your Creator. Learn to know the heart of God in the words of God *(Disce cor Dei in verbis Dei)."*[18] A medieval writer, Gottfried d'Admont, continues this reflection in a Christological key, taking as his starting point John's description of the disciple whom Jesus loved reclining on Jesus' breast at the Last Supper (cf. John 13:25): "The breast of Jesus is Sacred Scripture *(Pectus Jesu Sacra Scriptura est).* . . . Those who love God

18. *Ep.,* IV.31 (PL 77, 706 A-B).

and desire to imitate Jesus must make an effort to know Sacred Scripture with the single intention of attaining in this way to a greater knowledge of God, that is, of discovering in it the heart of God."[19] From Sacred Scripture one ascends to the interior knowledge of Jesus, at his "breast"; and from Jesus' breast, from his heart, to the heart of God! But problems immediately arise.

The Relation between the Two Aspects

a. If the Bible is both a human word and the Word of God, the fundamental question cannot be avoided: What is the relationship between the two dimensions, between the meaning intended by the human author and the meaning willed by God? Are they identical? At first glance, we could be tempted to believe this. But then all the insistence of the Fathers of the Church on distinguishing with precision *"history and Spirit"* in reading the Bible (cf. the title of Henri de Lubac's work on Origen), and their invitation to the reader to raise himself, in the words of St. Gregory the Great, "from *history to the mystery*,"[20] would be nothing but a pious illusion. Let us then ask the question clearly, at least of exegetes who admit the divine inspiration of Scripture: What relation do they perceive between that which they call the "sense intended by the author" and the plan of God? This is the problem, almost ignored today, of the hermeneutic value of inspiration. To this question, the majority of exegetes would probably reply, "The fact that the text is inspired has nothing to do with the mode of interpreting Scripture, and it does not have to have anything to do with it, certainly not in scientific exegesis." Basically, for the practice of interpretation, inspiration is useless. But if this is the case, we can tranquilly abandon the doctrine of inspiration as a vestige of the past. At most we would attribute to it the merit of having heightened the authority of the text, since, as Mons. Albert Descamps once wrote, everything that the human author wrote

---

19. *Hom.*, 51 (PL 174, 339 B-C); see also St. Thomas Aquinas, *In Ps.* 21.11: "*Per cor Christi intelligitur Sacra Scriptura quae manifestat Cor Christi*" (Ed. Parmensis, XIV, 221).

20. "Ab historia in mysterium surgit," *In Ez.*, I.6.3 (PL 76, 829 C).

down, God made his own. All that? Certainly. But nothing but that? This would imply a reversal of roles: God would be reduced to nothing but the guarantor of whatever man says. In this case, the Word of God is limited and locked into the limited horizon of a human word, and this is at the very least paradoxical. It would suffice, then, to analyze with exactitude the text of the human author in order to know God's intention. Obviously, the exegetes gain a lot: they are the arbiters of the theological situation — we, the exegetes!

But then, if the meaning of the Word of God must be reduced to the historical meaning of the human word set down in the Bible, we would have to call the Fathers' continual wonderment at the depths of Sacred Scripture naïve. We recall, for example, St. Augustine's cry in the *Confessions:* "What wonderful profundity there is in your words! . . . The depth is amazing, my God, the depth is amazing."[21] Where do we find this "profundity" of the words of God (*eloquia tua*) if everything is already contained and expressed in the words of men, which we can study with philological, literary, and historical analysis? After all, we have before us only the texts of these human authors.

We have to acknowledge that here, at the very origins, something is not right; something is structurally false. And the fact that all this does not provoke astonishment, unease, a question, shows to what extent scientific exegesis has become for many a profession, the sole requirements of which are competence in the philological, literary, and historical sciences. The only criteria of its status are those that human *reason* can discover in the text and in the age that gave rise to it. Exegesis is not, therefore, a "science of *faith.*" Someone might object that these extreme positions are the logical consequence of the modern doctrine of inspiration: they say that the biblical author is the instrument of God. But what is meant by this? Usually, attention is focused solely on the "instrument," the human author, and on the literary formulation that he, as "true author" (DV 11:1), gave to the text. The encyclical certainly affirmed the fact that he was also the "instrument

---

21. "Mira profunditas eloquiorum tuorum . . . mira profunditas, Deus meus, mira profunditas!" Confessions, XII, 14, 17 (PL 32, 832) (English translation: H. Chadwick [Oxford: Oxford University Press 1992], slightly modified).

of the Holy Spirit" (DAS 15; EB 556), but it did not explain this at all. This does not seem to worry the exegetes. If, in a book of the Bible, there is something greater or deeper, it escapes them and does not concern them. If God's plan expresses itself in the text, they ignore it. What we can know of these books is fixed in discrete segments, in texts produced by men in various epochs of the past. The contemporary commentator knows only isolated stones, but does not know that they are part of a mosaic! He is convinced that there is "nothing beyond that which is written," the exact opposite of what Origen, for example, thought. For him, the truth of Scripture is unutterable.[22]

We have lost a sense of the "mystery" of the Word of God, a sense of its unity and transcendence. If, by force of habit, we sometimes repeat the theory of the sacred writer-"instrument," we think rather of the fact that he was an instrument of the culture of his time and the historical expression of his environment: he is no longer the instrument of Revelation. In fact, the doctrine of *inspiration* has been eliminated.

b. How did we come to this? First of all, we must realize that today, a growing unease afflicts biblical exegesis. We glimpse a sign of this in the fact that there is much talk of the "Bible" today, but not of "Sacred Scripture," that is, of the Bible as an *inspired* book. In order to understand this situation, we must cast a glance backward into the past, and briefly retrace the evolution of the theory of inspiration in modern theology.[23] The seventeenth century was "the golden age, the classical age of the study of Inspiration" in the Church (Mangenot). In the last century, however, the problems raised by historical criticism challenged the theology of inspiration in a new way. Confronted by rationalism, the Church insisted on two points: the *divine* origin of Sacred Scripture (hence the importance attrib-

22. Cf. Origen, *Philocalie, 1-20, sur les Écritures.* Introduction and notes by M. Harl (SC 302) (Paris: Cerf: 1983), esp. pp. 151-53: "the truth is 'unutterable': beyond 'that which is written.'"

23. Cf. the contributions of A. M. Artola, *De la revelación a la inspiración: Los orígenes de la moderna teología católica sobre la inspiración bíblica* (Valencia/Bilbao: 1983); and two articles on the modern period: "De 'Dios autor de los libros sagrados' a la 'Escritura como obra literaria,'" in *EstEcl* 56 (1981): 651-69; "Treinta años de reflexión sobre la inspiración bíblica," in *EstBíb* 47 (1989): 363-415.

uted to the formula *Deus auctor Scripturae* already in Vatican I: DH 3006), and its absolute truth, or inerrancy, forcefully affirmed from Leo XIII's encyclical *Providentissimus Deus* (1893) onward.

Above all, it was this "obsession with *inerrancy*" (A. M. Artola) that sparked the famous "biblical question" during the dark period of modernism. Pius XII can be credited with putting an end to the question with his encyclical, *Divino Afflante Spiritu* (1943).

This marked the beginning of a new era. Stress was laid on the *historical* study of the Bible and on the *critical* search for the single *literal sense* intended by the human author. The theological principle of inspiration was certainly reaffirmed as an acquisition of the past (it was even proclaimed in the title of the encyclical); but what did it mean for the work of the exegete? It should have been a vital principle if it was to grow and mature with the problems of the time. No effort at all was made to rethink it in depth, in this new context dominated by historical interest. Hence, the insistence on historical exegesis became the nurturing ground for that which provoked the crisis of inspiration. In fact, the years after the encyclical's publication saw the first criticisms of the then-current theologies of inspiration. This rapidly intensified after the Council, to such a degree that a book was published with the tone of a manifesto: in the title of the work, the author announced "the end of the theology of inspiration."[24] In our day, exegetes certainly continue to study the religious doctrine of the biblical writings from both a historical and theological point of view, but they do not themselves feel that the inspiration of Scripture makes any sort of demand on them. They no longer pose the classical problem of the spiritual sense of Scripture; the tradition of a properly *Christian* interpretation of the Bible has been judged inopportune.

c. Vatican II opened new horizons, but they were not taken advantage of, or even seen. We will highlight three points that allow us to see the

---

24. O. Loretz, *Das Ende der Inspirationstheologie: Chancen eines Neubeginns*, 2 vols. (Stuttgart: 1974, 1976). More recently, H. Haag espoused a similar position in "Streit um die Bibel unter fünf Päpsten," in *ThQ* 170 (1990): 241-53; cf. p. 252: "Inspiration is a theme which — at least in its traditional form — no longer concerns us, and that we can consign into the faithful hands of colleagues in other disciplines, for example fundamental or dogmatic theology."

complexities and nuances of the Council's position. This complexity is understandable, since the redaction of *Dei Verbum* involved the difficult search for a new balance.

We note first the novelty of the use of the word "author" in *Dei Verbum*. In continuity with Vatican I, the Constitution affirms that the sacred books "have God as their author" (II:I). But more than before, this formula must be understood here analogously, since in the same context and for the first time in a document of the Magisterium, the word "author" is also applied to the sacred writers. The Constitution insists on this point: when the biblical authors wrote down their text under the action of God, they acted "as true authors" (the contribution of *Divino Afflante Spiritu* is integrated here). But then the question arises: What is the relationship between *Deus auctor* and the *hagiographus auctor*? Do they both mean to say the same thing? Then why the reduplication? We mention another consequence of this insistence on the human author. From the value given to what is *written*, one could deduce that the conciliar doctrine regarding inspiration underwent "an important transformation," orienting itself toward the *linguistic sciences*.[25] Is this true? The linguistic sciences are human sciences: they cannot offer a theological explanation of inspiration, which is an action that has its source in God. Precisely because of inspiration, it remains perennially true that the sacred books "have *God* as their author." The *Deus auctor* cannot simply be reduced to the *hagiographus auctor*; the intention of the first exceeds that of the second. A reading that wished to abandon this principle in order to study the Scripture simply as the literary and historical work of a human author would be reductive. It would have to be filled out and rectified by other aspects of a theological order, highlighted by the conciliar Constitution.

This leads us to our second point. One of the Council's most novel contributions is that of having posited a strict relationship between *inspiration* and *truth*. Of course, it arrived at this point only at the end of a difficult journey (from 1961 to 1965), but in the final text, the pre-conciliar problem of the absolute inerrancy of all the propositions of the Bible was completely overcome. This does not mean that the idea of the truth of the

25. A. M. Artola, "De 'Dios autor de los libros sagrados' . . . ," p. 664.

Bible was abandoned; to the contrary! But the "truth" is now seen on another plane, no longer that of historical truth alone. As the Constitution says, since the books of Scripture are *inspired*, they teach "that truth which God wanted put into sacred writings for the sake of our salvation" (11:2). Therefore, like the *heavenly book* shown to Daniel in his apocalyptic vision (Dan 10:21), the book of the Sacred Scripture must be for us "the Book of Truth"! The truth, understood in this biblical sense, here designates divine Revelation, as it does already in chapter 1 of the Constitution. The reality of "salvation," too, belongs to the order of Revelation. The joining of the two terms, "truth" and "salvation," leads us back to a formula from the previous redaction: "the truth which saves." This can be found elsewhere in the texts of the Council (*veritas salutaris, salutaris veritas*: GS 28:2; DV 7). Thus we can see that in this perspective, the level of the human sciences, including the linguistic sciences, has clearly been exceeded. This holds true also for the level of the merely historical truth of the biblical narratives. The "truth" of Scripture is the truth of its profound sense, the divine and revealing sense of the Word of God, which goes "beyond" the literal and historical sense of the individual texts because it unveils the plan of salvation, the mystery of Revelation.

Here, in n. 11 of *Dei Verbum*, we discover again the problem posed by the two preceding sections of this article: the Bible as human word and the Word of God, and the relation between these two aspects. In the following paragraph of the Constitution, the distinction between the two points of view is made explicit, as we demonstrated elsewhere, in a detailed analysis of n. 12.[26] From the beginning, the text obliges us to distinguish two levels:

+ on the one hand, "what *God* has wished to communicate to us . . . [and] which *God* had thought well to manifest through the medium of their words";
+ on the other hand, that which the *sacred writers* truly wanted to say.

These two levels, which are not identical, are taken up again and developed in the following paragraphs. Paragraph 12:2 indicates how much must be done "for the correct understanding of what the sacred author wanted

---

26. Cf. above, the last article cited in footnote 3.

to assert" (we find here a reference to Pius XII's encyclical). Paragraph 12:3 begins with "But" (so there is a certain opposition between the two): it explains that Scripture must be read and *interpreted* "with its divine authorship in mind"; hence, the charism of inspiration is recalled here in a hermeneutic perspective (that is, with a view to *interpretation*). If in 12:2 the Council invited us to seek out the meaning the *sacred writer* intended to express, it no longer says, as the encyclical, that this is "the supreme law of exegesis." In the same sense, we observe that in that paragraph, *Dei Verbum* does not even use the word "interpretation" with reference to philological and historical exegesis. The verb "interpret" appears only in 12:3, in connection with the mention of the *Spirit* and the *inspired* character of Scripture, and also with a reminder of the *unity* of the whole of Scripture and of the living *Tradition* of the Church.

We will stress a third point: the interpretation of Scripture "in the sacred Spirit in which it was written" (12:3). Of course, this principle was invoked even before Vatican II, but in a secularized fashion: "in the spirit (not capitalized) of the human author." This is obviously not wrong, but it is unilateral. Read solely thus, in a manner contrary to the entire Tradition, the principle would reduce the Bible to a mere historical document. In DV 12:3, *Spiritu* is capitalized and refers to the Holy Spirit, he who *inspired* Sacred Scripture. So the perspective must be inverted, no longer simply from above to below (and *a fortiori* not only in the horizontal perspective of history), but also vertically, from below to above. This means that we must consider the text of Scripture as the instrument of *Revelation*, the expression of the *mystery* of the Word of God, which expresses itself in it; this Word transcends history. The biblical text evokes the mystery because it is inspired by the Holy Spirit, precisely he who makes the whole Bible into one book, the instrument of Revelation, the instrument of the Word of God.

As we move from one paragraph to another of *Dei Verbum*, from 12:2 to 12:3, the shift in perspective is clear: from a primarily human, philological, and historical point of view (in 12:2), we move in 12:3 to a much more theological, ecclesial, and eschatological vision of "Sacred Scripture," because the latter is presented to Christians and to the Church as the Word of God, the "Book of Truth," the text inspired by the Holy Spirit. Ultimately, the true sense of Scripture, if it is read "in the Spirit," is its spiritual sense made manifest in the Church.[27]

What Does Scripture Have to Say about This?

One could object that these principles of interpretation are a theological teaching of the Council and of the Church's tradition, but they are foreign to the teaching of the Bible itself. We wish to demonstrate, to the contrary, that in its essentials, this doctrine already belongs to Scripture. The authors of the biblical writings affirm that their message was *inspired* by the Spirit of God, and remains open to the *mystery* of God that transcends them.

In the epistle to the Romans, Paul exclaims, "O the depth of the riches and wisdom and knowledge of God! How unsearchable are his judgments and inscrutable his ways!" (Rom 11:33). In the epistle's conclusion, the Apostle speaks to the Romans of the "revelation of the mystery which was kept secret for long ages but is now disclosed" in the proclamation of Jesus Christ. However, it is paradoxical that, for Paul, the proclamation of the gospel was accomplished in his time "through the prophetic writings ... according to the command of the eternal God" (Rom 16:25-26). Thus, in the prophetic message was already hidden the mystery of salvation which was later to be revealed in the gospel. We find an analogous conception in the letter to the Ephesians: Paul asks the Christians to pray for him in the Spirit, so that he might be granted "a bold word to proclaim the *mystery* of the *gospel*" (Eph 6:19). Thus, the gospel is not only the kerygma, the good news of salvation: the expression "the *mystery* of the gospel" (*tò mystérion toû euangelíou*), which is apocalyptic in origin, invites us to see in it also the unveiling of the Plan of salvation.

27. These indications of the Council are related to what many contemporary authors are saying on various levels, including philosophy, literary criticism, and theology. Besides the work of Ricoeur, cf. also L. Lavelle, *La Parole et l'écriture* (Paris: Presses Universitaires de France, 1947), pp. 27-41: "The Gap between Thought and Language"; pp. 159-71: "The Eternal in the Temporal"; R. Welleck and A. Warren, *Theory of Literature*, 3rd ed. (London: Cape, 1966); L. Bouyer, *Gnosis: La connaisance de Dieu dans l'Écriture* (Paris: Cerf, 1988), esp. pp. 175-76.

The same theme appears again in the two letters of Peter. The second letter insists that "no prophecy ever came by the impulse of man, but men moved by the Holy Spirit spoke *on behalf of God*" (2 Pet 1:21). The first letter tells us that the prophets "inquired what circumstances or time was indicated by the *Spirit of Christ within them* when they predicted the sufferings of Christ and the glory that was to follow them." The author explains, "It was revealed to them that they were serving not themselves but you [the Christians]," and this fulfillment was "announced to you by those who preached the *gospel* through the *Holy Spirit*" (1 Pet 1:11-12). The Spirit of Christ already gave the prophets an implicit knowledge of the gospel, which is the "sense" of Scripture.

John's teaching follows the same lines. During the Last Supper, Jesus says to his disciples, "I am the Truth" (John 14:6). Nonetheless, he announces just a little later that the Spirit of Truth must still come "to guide them into all the truth" (cf. John 16:13). Without the action of the Spirit, they cannot really *comprehend* the "truth" of Jesus. The same idea is expressed in the final verse of John's Gospel: "The world would not be able to 'contain' [or 'comprehend'?] the books that would be written" (21:25). The meaning of these words has been debated, but the best interpretation remains that of Origen: this impossibility refers to the greatness and spiritual depth of the facts reported. "Man cannot comprehend and express in its fullness the meaning of the words and actions of Christ."[28] Without the Spirit of truth, without the Spirit given by Christ himself (cf. John 20:22), man is incapable of comprehending "the mystery of the gospel," the "truth" of Scripture, the profound "meaning" of the Word of God. This is a Christian hermeneutical principle that we absolutely cannot do without.

This interpretive principle was given a particularly noteworthy formulation in two fundamental texts of St. Gregory the Great. In both texts, we find the term "mystery," as in the Pauline verses cited above. The first is one to which St. Thomas Aquinas also refers when he expounds his theory of the sense of Scripture (*S.Th.* I.1.10):

---

28. Cf. my article, "Le témoin qui demeure: Le disciple que Jésus aimait," in *Bib* 67 (1986): 343-59, in which I indicate the main texts of Origen on this theme.

Sacred Scripture incomparably transcends every knowledge and every doctrine . . . because it in some way grows together with those who read it (*aliquo modo cum legentibus crescit*): . . . It transcends all knowledge and all doctrine by its very manner of expressing itself, since with one and the same expression, through the narrative of the text, it reveals a mystery (*dum narrat textum, prodit mysterium*). . . .[29]

In the other passage we cited earlier, St. Gregory reminds the believer that, in order to understand a story in the Bible, "he must raise himself from the story to the mystery (*ab historia in mysterium surgit*)."[30] These two texts summarize all that is essential in the patristic doctrine of the senses of Scripture: the Bible does not only contain the telling of a history, and it reveals to us the mystery of salvation because it is for us the book of Revelation. It is at this level, the level of the mystery, that it reveals its profound sense, "the sense given by the Spirit," which the whole Christian tradition has always sought to discover in Scripture.[31]

The Unity of the Whole of Scripture

From the theological principle we have just described flows a fundamental consequence for interpretation: the Bible as a whole forms a unity. Beyond work on this or that text, which remains the exegete's primary task, he is subject to a vaster principle of unity which, beyond the particular texts, the different books and the two Testaments, gathers into itself the whole of Scripture, which is centered on Christ. In this we have a classical doctrine of the whole Christian tradition, which, however, is in the course of being abandoned by modern scientific exegesis. It has rightly been said that for the latter, the unity of the Bible is "an obsolete postulate" (J. Ratzinger).[32]

29. *Mor.*, 20.1 (PL 76, 135 B-D). See the commentary on this text in P. C. Bori, *L'interpretazione infinita: L'ermeneutica cristiana antica e le sue trasformazioni* (Bologna: Il Mulino, 1987), pp. 27-41.

30. *In Ez.*, I.6.3 (PL 76, 829 C).

31. Cf. H. de Lubac, *L'Écriture dans la Tradition* (Paris: Aubier-Montaigne, 1966), pp. 189-202: "The Sense Given by the Spirit."

32. See on p. 6.

Nevertheless — and this is important — it is being rediscovered today to an equal degree in other schools of contemporary exegesis, which are more interested in a thematic and theological reading of Scripture.

Just one example. Various recent studies on the figure of Mary have shown that already in the gospels, she is not described merely as a Jewish woman of the first century, the wife of Joseph and the mother of Jesus. In the passages of the New Testament, she is presented as the woman who evokes a symbolic figure of the prophetic tradition, Daughter Zion, the Virgin Israel. In this progressive movement of symbolization, already in the gospels, Mary is gradually integrated "into the mystery of Christ and the Church," as the Council desired (LG ch. VIII); but the "mystery of Christ and the Church" is that of the Covenant, which includes the whole of Scripture.[33] In this ever-more-expansive context, the person of the mother of Jesus is at last presented to us — according to the admirable formula of a medieval author — as "the fulfillment of the Synagogue, and the new beginning of the Holy Church."[34] Undeniably, this interpretation, which identifies Mary's mission with that of "Daughter Zion" in the global context of all of Scripture, represents considerable progress from the hermeneutic and theological points of view.

The doctrine of the unity of Scripture was certainly already present to the spirit of the authors of the New Testament. They interpret the Old Testament in the light of their Christian experience, but they also seek reciprocally to understand the mystery of Jesus by reading Scripture. A detail of vocabulary demonstrates their conviction: the use of the expression "Scripture" in the singular. We find it, for example, in John's account of the Passion, where the evangelist tells us that on the cross, in the last moment of Jesus' life, "Scripture" was perfectly fulfilled (cf. John 19:28). After the Resurrection, Jesus himself said to his disciples, "Everything written *about me* in the law of Moses and the prophets and the psalms must be fulfilled" (Luke 24:44). The evangelist continues, "Then he opened their minds to understand the Scriptures" (24:45). The expression *aperuit illis sensum ut intelli-*

---

33. See my work, *Mary in the Mystery of the Covenant* (New York: Alba House, 1992).

34. Gerhoh of Reichersberg, *Liber de Gloria et honore Filii Hominis*, 10.1 (PL 194, 1105 B): "*Consummatio Synagogae . . . et Ecclesiae sanctae nova inchoatio.*"

gerent Scripturas became for medieval monastic theology one of the basic texts for biblically founding the search for the spiritual sense of Scripture.[35] To illustrate the doctrine of the unity of Scripture, Fr. de Lubac gathered an impressive dossier of ancient testimonies, both in *Histoire et Esprit* [History and Spirit] (on Origen) and in *Medieval Exegesis*. We will cite just one text, the famous formula of Hugo of St. Victor: "*Omnis Scriptura divina unus liber est, et ille liber unus Christus est.*"[36] We recall that the same teaching was taken up in the conciliar Constitution *Dei Verbum*, when it says that in order to interpret Scripture "in the same Spirit in which it was written," we must devote attention "to the content and unity of the whole of Scripture" (12:3). This unity, the Council tells us again in chapter 4, comes from the fact that God is the one who inspired the books of both Testaments; for this reason, they express a single plan of salvation. God disposed them in such a way that "the New should be hidden in the Old and . . . the Old should be made manifest in the New" (DV 16).

On the other hand — and this is in some ways even more surprising — the same principle of the unity of the Bible is being rediscovered today from a rigorously hermeneutic perspective, on the purely literary level of the concatenation of texts. We refer to the recent work of Northrop Frye, *The Great Code: The Bible and Literature*,[37] which was presented in *Biblica* by P. J. Cahill in an article entitled, precisely, "The Unity of the Bible."[38] Thus, it is

35. Cf. P. Dumontier, *S. Bernard et la Bible* (Paris: Desclée de Brouwer, 1953), pp. 89-96; H. de Lubac, *Medieval Exegesis: The Four Senses of Scripture*, vol. 2, trans. Edward M. Macierowski (Grand Rapids: Eerdmans, 2000), pp. 174-75; M. Magrassi, "La Bibbia nei chiostri di Cluny e di Citeaux," in C. Vagaggini et al., *Bibbia e spiritualità* (Rome: Paoline, 1967), pp. 178-244 (p. 211).

36. *De arca Dei morali*, II.8 (PL 176, 642). We add two more celebrated formulae of the patristic age: "*Inseminatus est ubique in Scripturis . . . Filius Dei*" [the Son of God is implanted everywhere throughout the Scriptures], St. Irenaeus of Lyons, *Adv. haer.* IV.10.1 (SC 100, 492); "*Lege libros omnes propheticos: non intellecto Christo, quid tam insipidum et fatuum invenies? Intellige ibi Christum: non solum sapit quod legis, sed etiam inebriat*" [Read all the prophetic books; and if Christ be not understood therein, what can you find so insipid and silly? Understand Christ in them, and what you read not only has a taste, but even inebriates you], St. Augustine, *In Io.*, tr. 9.3 (PL 35, 1459).

37. London-New York: Routledge Kegan Paul, Harcourt Brace Jovanovich, 1982.

38. *Bib* 65 (1984): 404-11.

not without reason that Cardinal Ratzinger, after having noted in his discussion of exegesis that the same principle already regulated Jewish exegesis, insists in his conclusion: "The first presupposition of all exegesis is that it takes the Bible as *one* book. If it does so, then it has already chosen for itself a position that is rooted in much more than the literary aspects of the text."[39]

The unity of the Bible transcends questions of history and of the genesis of texts. It consists in the fact that the Scripture as Word of God expresses the divine plan of salvation; this finds its center in Christ, "who is both the mediator and the fullness of all revelation" (DV 2). For us, then, Scripture is fundamentally the instrument of revelation; the human authors who wrote the Bible were inspired by God precisely to this effect. Moreover, it is precisely in this that the hermeneutic value of inspiration consists.

What can we draw from this regarding our manner of doing exegesis? If Scripture is the Word of God, if it reveals the mystery of salvation, it requires a modality of interpretation that goes beyond the purely historical, philological, and literary aspects of the texts. The profound meaning of Scripture, its "truth," can only be discovered "beyond what is written," on the level of mystery and faith. We will investigate this more closely in the second part.

The Interpretation of Sacred Scripture: A Science of Faith

The Problem

Let us begin once more from our initial question: What is the epistemological status of biblical exegesis? In his article cited above,[40] Romano Guardini answered: it belongs to the "science of faith" (*Glaubenswissenschaft*), that is, to theology. Thus he anticipated the Council, which would say the same thing thirty years later.

---

39. Above, p. 29. For a critical presentation of this principle, see W. Gross, "Einheit der Bibel?," in *ThQ* 170 (1990): 304-6.

40. See p. 34 n. 13.

Doubtless, two objections could be made against this viewpoint. First, if this is the case, exegesis is insufficiently distinguished from other areas of theology and runs the risk of being subordinated to dogmatic or moral theology, or spirituality. To this objection, it is enough to respond that exegesis is only a species within a genus: on its own level, it must retain its autonomy. But, as Blondel writes, "autonomy must not become the autarchy of history";[41] he repeatedly warned against the sort of exegesis that he called "separate."[42] Exegesis is not simply a historical or philological science. It is a science of *interpretation* applied to Sacred Scripture; because of this, it is and must be a *theological* science, integrated into the greater whole that is theology. And since theology is the *intellectus fidei,* or *fides quarens intellectum,* exegesis, too, must be a "science of faith," a science by means of which the exegete seeks a deeper understanding of the *sense* of Scripture from the starting point of faith, and a deeper understanding of his faith in the light of Scripture. It follows that exegesis, provided that its relative autonomy within its own methodology is respected, should not conflict with dogma, moral theology, or spirituality. To the contrary, it will enter into a dialectical relationship with these three ecclesial disciplines; this relationship will doubtless provoke tensions, but these ought always to tend toward a harmonious resolution. If, according to the Council, exegesis must be "as it were, the soul of sacred theology" (DV 24), exegesis obviously must be situated within theology, since it is as the soul in the body. Now, this is possible only if the interpreter of the Bible, the exegete, is also a theologian who listens to the other areas of theology, and not only a specialist in biblical philology, ancient history, or literary theories.

The other difficulty is more fundamental: post-Enlightenment modern

41. Letter of Blondel to Wehrlé, April 6, 1903; quoted in R. Fontan, "Maurice Blondel et la crise moderniste (années 1902-1903) d'après la correspondance du philosophe," in *BLitE* (1977): 103-44 (here, p. 131).

42. Cf. R. Marlé, *Au coeur de la crise moderniste: Le dossier inédit d'une controverse* (Paris: Aubier-Montaigne, 1960), p. 114, in a letter from Blondel to Wehrlé: "'Separate' exegesis is an inexhaustible source of doubts and dangerous preoccupations." See also "History and Dogma," in *The Letter on Apologetics & History and Dogma,* trans. A. Dru and I. Trethowan (Grand Rapids: Eerdmans, 1994), p. 286: "A separate dogmatic theology, a separate exegesis, a separate history, necessarily remain incomplete."

culture commonly holds faith and reason to be incompatible. To speak of a "science of faith" seems to be a contradiction. Does this mean that theology, which seeks the *intellectus fidei*, cannot be called a science? The same apparent dilemma arises in exegesis: if the exegete is a believer, we are told that he lets himself be influenced by his beliefs and does not engage in scientific work. If he wants to be scientific, he cannot take his faith into account, because to do the contrary would not respect a fundamental rule of scientific work in the modern age: the rigorous *autonomy* of reason. Everyone knows that this old objection has its source in the rationalism of the eighteenth century. With regard to exegesis, we can trace it back above all to Spinoza (in his *Tractatus Theologico-Politicus*), who was celebrated as "the initiator of biblical criticism" (A. Lods) and one of the "founders of modern exegesis" (L. Brunschvicg). According to Spinoza, exegetical research should follow only the norms dictated by reason — concretely, the rules of philology and the science of history. It ought to ignore everything that is told to us by faith and ecclesial tradition, and refuse every opening toward transcendence.

However, before responding to this difficulty, we will examine R. Guardini's position more closely.

The "Science of Faith" according to R. Guardini

a. The starting point of his thought is the epistemological principle we made reference to above: the requisite method for attaining knowledge of an object must be conformed to the nature of the object under examination. This is why, in part one of this article, we spent so much time responding to the question regarding the object: What is the Bible? For the question regarding the subject, which we take up now, Guardini's response is perfectly clear: "Faith is the correlative cognitive attitude to the Word of God" (p. 70).[43] Further on, he writes, "The proper nature of the sacred text remains excluded [*ausgeschaltet*] in the strict sense of the word as long as the appropriate attitude is lacking: faith. Whoever considers the sacred

---

43. The numbers in parentheses refer to the pages in the Italian version (see n. 13 above).

text from a merely historical point of view does not at all see in it the true and proper object. He sees only exterior phenomena, psychological contexts, words with various philological and cultural meanings" (p. 71). But the Word of God as such remains hidden to him: it cannot be comprehended except in the light of faith. Guardini demonstrates this using an absolutely essential word in biblical revelation: "grace." (We recall what we said above regarding the words "full of grace" as they are applied to Mary.) In all of Guardini's reflections, we discern the influence of the Pauline text he cites repeatedly: "The things of the Spirit of God . . . can only be judged spiritually. The spiritual man judges all things, but himself cannot be judged by anyone" (1 Cor 2:14-15). No less important is what we read in the letter to the Hebrews: "Faith is . . . the means to know things not seen" (Heb 11:1). It gives us a real certainty, because it is a manner of seeing the invisible (cf. Heb 11:27). On the level of the invisible, which is the level of properly spiritual realities, the historical method as such can do nothing.

Scripture, as the Word of God, is in fact very different from a merely historical document that informs us about Israel's and the early Christians' past; it is an inspired text revealing God's action in history. As the Word of God, it can be received only in faith.

b. Guardini continues, "The science *of faith* deals precisely with this: the Word of God understood *in faith*" (p. 80). But isn't this affirmation a pure paradox? In what sense can we speak *here* of science? Doesn't an entirely "scientific" exegesis already exist today? Are we then to ignore it? We cannot deny that Guardini issues a severe judgment on such "scientific" exegesis. It is certainly not the science of faith he proposes: "Our biblical science," he writes, "is predominantly historicist. A scientific understanding of Sacred Scripture coincides in great measure with understanding it historically" (p. 83). But with this method, we run the risk precisely of losing that which constitutes the essential and permanent element of exegesis: the theological dimension. Guardini adds, in a lapidary passage: "That which is properly theological threatens to elude our grasp. . . . We risk losing present-ness (*die Gegenwärtigkeit*): the 'today' in which both theologians and listeners are placed. In its 'yesterday,' historicism loses both the eternal and the 'today'" (p. 83).

Nevertheless and in spite of all appearances, according to Guardini, we can develop an authentic "science of faith." That is, we can do the work of exegesis within faith while at the same time respecting the strict laws of scientific research. In fact, true science consists in the rational elaboration of human knowledge, for example in the area of mathematics, physics, philology, history, or literary history. There is no reason why such an operation could not be applied also to religious knowledge, as the knowledge of faith which is expressed in the Bible. If a theologian wishes to undertake a theological exegesis of the Bible, the scientific value of his work, says Guardini, is determined by two conditions: "first, by the robustness of the faith-knowledge he has of revelation, and only secondarily by the robustness of his conceptual, interpretative and elaborative capacities" (p. 86).

We are happy to note that Guardini's ideas — which we have laid out here in a very summary fashion — regarding the scientific value of exegesis in faith, were recently confirmed and further developed by a renowned specialist in the philosophy of science, Jean Ladrière, in his reflection on theology as a science in the twentieth century.[44] He says that theology, unlike mathematics or physics, for example, is a "hermeneutical science." This is also the case, we would add, with biblical exegesis. As a positive science, theology has as its object "the deciphering of texts, the meaning of which is not or is no longer immediately accessible," and it implicates "in an essential manner the category of 'sense.'" It is "an effort to understand a 'given,'" an effort that cannot be made except "in the experience of faith." So what is, then, "the sort of scientific-ness proper to theology"? Ladrière boldly states that it is fundamentally the same as that of the other sciences, and explains, "The theological effort is an effort at intelligibility sustained by a desire for radicality, which is what confers upon it precisely a 'scientific' character. It cannot be radical without at the same time wanting itself to be critical, systematic, and dynamic" (p. 238). He himself explains how we are to understand the third condition: "The dynamic of theology is a tension that incessantly runs the length of its hermeneutical effort and guides it toward a 'saturation of meaning'" (p. 239). Of course we are dealing here with a "limit-marker, whose inaccessibility is marked by the dimension of the mys-

---

44. J. Ladrière, "Postface" to the work of T. Tshibangu, *La théologie comme science au XXe siècle* (Kinshasa: Presses Universitaires du Zaire, 1980), pp. 229-44.

tery that belongs properly to faith." Nevertheless, theology must orient itself precisely in this direction, and it is from the demand for an ever-more-
adequate comprehension that "it draws its proper dynamism" (p. 239).

These principles are liberating when applied to exegesis. We draw attention to the extent to which the theory that understands the interpretation of Scripture as the search for a *"growing* saturation of *meaning"* opens
us to the problem of the relationship between Scripture and Tradition. It
draws us closer, too, to Gadamer's principle of *Wirkungsgeschichte*, and
even more so to recent works on the "infinite interpretation" of the Bible.
These are but an effort at rationally systematizing that which was already
practiced in ancient exegesis, both Jewish and Christian.[45]

Michael Theobald's Critical Reaction

Various recent studies have examined Guardini's principles for the interpretation of Scripture. It cannot be said that exegetes received these principles favorably. We take the clearest example: Theobald's critical analysis of
them in 1987.[46] The title already speaks volumes: "The Autonomy of Historical Criticism, Expression of Incredulity or Theological Necessity?"
Theobald's criticisms of Guardini oddly evoke those which Loisy made of
Blondel at the beginning of the twentieth century.

After identifying the main sources of Guardini's thought (the Alexan-
drine tradition, Plato, Kierkegaard, Barth), Theobald confronts the central
principle of Guardini's epistemology head-on (the correspondence between object and subject in the act of knowing), as well as the fact that

45. For Jewish exegesis, see D. Banon, *La lecture infinie: Les voies de l'interprétation
midrashique* (Paris: Éditions du Seuil, 1987). For Christian exegesis (especially in the Latin
tradition), P. C. Bori, *L'interpretazione infinita* (cited in note 29); the author appears to have
taken this title from a text of John Scotus Erigena: "The interpretation of Holy Scripture is
infinite" (*Sacrae Scripturae interpretatio infinita est*), *De divisione naturae*, II.20 (PL 122, 560
A). We recall that the work of P. C. Bori (cf. the subtitle) is the study of "the ancient Christian hermeneutic and its transformations" (especially beginning with the Scholastics). He
presents a noteworthy analysis of the text of St. Gregory the Great (*Mor.*, 20.1, on the
"growth" of Scripture), which we cited above.

46. See above, note 14.

Guardini admits a "hierarchy of degrees of the real." According to Theobald, the latter points to the Platonism inspiring Guardini's thought. This is a stunning conclusion: Distinguishing the words of men and the Word of God in Scripture is supposed to be Platonism? This distinction does not come from Platonic idealism, but from biblical revelation, and was embraced continuously by the whole Judeo-Christian tradition up to Vatican II. Nonetheless, Theobald clearly is interested only in the human dimension of the biblical texts, their literary and historical aspect. From this restricted point of view, he obviously had an easy time chiding Guardini in 1987 for ignoring *Formgeschichte* (Guardini was writing in 1928!), not discussing literary genre, and giving too much credit to the historical value of the gospels. His most basic criticism is, however, the following: almost scandalized, Theobald affirms that for Guardini (likened here to Barth), "historical truth . . . cannot be the ultimate and decisive criterion for the interpretation of Scripture" (p. 25).

Without a doubt, Guardini adamantly affirmed this. But *can* we make of it a reproach? For Theobald, on the other hand, the ultimate criterion of exegesis is, precisely, historical truth. So we have reached the heart of the problem. At this point, a single question suffices, and the question is decisive: What exactly are we to understand by the term *"interpretation* of Scripture"? Is it simply a *historical* discipline? Or is it rather, as Jean Ladrière says, a *hermeneutical* science? Is the "truth" that is sought in exegesis merely the truth of *history,* or is it not, on a deeper level, the truth and therefore the sense of *revelation?*[47] Or again, when we are dealing with *interpreting* the *inspired* text of the Bible, a text written in faith, mustn't a special kind of hermeneutics, the "science of faith," be brought into play? It is true that, for certain critical spirits, speaking of the "inspiration" of the Bible or of faith in a scientific discussion makes no sense and provokes laughter. Nevertheless, this is precisely the unavoidable question today: What is the epistemological status of biblical exegesis among believers? This is the whole problem of the *Christian* exegesis of the Bible. Left to themselves,

---

47. This was the vision of the Fathers of the Church: the search for the "truth" of Scripture was the search for its "sense." See for example this text of Zeno of Verona: "Go ahead, reader, call forth the sense, you will find the truth" [*"Age, excita sensum, lector, invenies veritatem"*], *Tractatus* II.4.3 (CCL 22, 159, 22).

philology and history remain powerless at this point; they must be situated firmly on a philosophical, hermeneutic, and theological plane. The refusal in our day to confront the problem on this deepest level creates a deep un-ease and threatens to give rise to growing conflict. This is the basic prob-lem we have to face. It demands that we give it priority of attention, more than to the many often boring and sterile discussions on questions of methodology in a rigorously scientific work.

Further on in his article, Theobald returns to that which he calls the "hierarchy of degrees of the real" in Guardini: the lower level in the Bible is that of the human and historical realities, whereas the higher level is that of "the spiritual (literally, pneumatic) dimension of the text, to which faith corresponds" (p. 25). Theobald observes with a certain sarcasm that such a distinction would of course be obvious in medieval thought, but he adds with great assurance, "in the modern age, biblical science has naturally abandoned this home" (p. 26). Too bad for it! We simply point out that in this "medieval home," people still lived from faith and at least kept their "homes" open to transcendence, listening to the Word of God; they obvi-ously were not yet familiar with the critical problems of today. Conversely, after the anthropocentric turn of modernity, the Bible is no longer the Word of God. The "home" into which positivistic science has confined it-self, though technically so well organized, no longer has any opening to-ward what is above; it is doubtless a very "functional" home, but a home closed in on itself, ignoring revelation and offering no answer to our great religious questions. It is the "home" of modern immanentism, as Blondel demonstrated so well.[48]

We are far from thinking that Guardini's reflection on biblical exegesis resolves all problems. Clearly, these reflections have to be continued and fur-ther developed, but those who criticize the lacunae of his exegetical *method* merely show that they have understood nothing of his intuition. His inten-

---

48. Cf. the subtitle of "History and Dogma": "The Philosophical Lacunae of Modern Exegesis." See also "Une des sources de la pensée moderne: L'évolution du spinozisme," in *Dialogues avec les philosophes* (Paris: Aubier, 1960), pp. 11-40; he writes that at the basis of the modern enterprise is "the desire to see the problem absolutely resolved by human effort alone" (p. 37); "the fundamental idea of Spinozism . . . is the notion of immanence: things bear their explanation and justification in themselves" (p. 31).

tion was not a method any more than was Blondel's in his dialogue with Loisy. The philosopher from Aix wrote to the exegete that the right of closing oneself into the methodical skepticism of the historian does not exist, and he added this luminous judgment: "The question is more complex: we lack the 'prolegomena to all future exegesis,' that is, a critical reflection on *the very conditions of a science of Revelation* and of all sacred literature. When such a systematic investigation is lacking, we risk stupidly losing that which is being questioned, or implicitly excluding *a priori* that which we think we are reserving for an *a posteriori* examination (and I will say immediately that, as I see it, this latter case applies to you)."[49] A "science of Revelation" (Blondel), a "science of faith" (Guardini): we can see how closely the positions of the philosopher and the theologian approach one another. Both pointed out, not what the exegetical *method* ought to be, but what the *conditions*, the necessary *prolegomena,* have to be, on the basis of which it is possible to develop a Christian exegesis today. By the latter we mean a theological interpretation of Sacred Scripture that is elaborated scientifically, but within faith.

Attempt at a Synthesis

In this last step of our exposition, we would like to formulate four basic theses that will help to better circumscribe or delineate what the epistemological status of Christian exegesis can and ought to be today.

a. Sacred Scripture is an inspired book, the Word of God addressed to all of us. It is, therefore, the *norma normans* for Christian faith and for theological research in the Church. For this reason, the Council said that it must be "as it were, the soul of sacred theology." Because of the primacy that the study of the Bible must hold in theology, the use of all the technical methods available to discover the *sense* the author wanted to give to his *text* is indispensable: historical context, philology, literary analysis, etc. Modern methodology has made enormous progress in this area, which obviously can no longer be ignored.

---

49. Long letter to Loisy of 15 February 1903; in R. Marlé, *Au coeur de la crise moderniste*, p. 90.

b. On the other hand, scientific exegesis has lost sight of the difference of "levels" between the written text and its profound sense, between the expression as it is formulated and that which Ricoeur calls the life of the text. Jean-Marie Sevrin recently said that the task of critical exegesis is that of shedding light on "the true sense of the text as text."[50] But this formula is profoundly ambiguous. Sevrin must have been aware of the ambiguity, because he adds that one never arrives at the origin of the threads from which the text is woven. Again with Ricoeur, we must ask the essential question: "What is a text?" Is the role of the exegete simply to explain the text, or must he also seek to understand it? The text is a symbol of thought, but it cannot express all the depth of the lived experience. The importance of the distinction between "explaining" and "understanding" in contemporary hermeneutics is well known. To affirm that the exegete's task is that of seeking out the sense of the text as text is to suppose that all the sense intended and experienced by the author is handed over to us in his formulation, in the statement itself. But is it by chance that the word "sense" also means direction, orientation, finality? It has rightly been noted that ultimately, the question of sense contains the hidden question of finality. "The sense of Scripture is its direction" (Paul Claudel). To forget this would be to rationalize the text, to confine its sense to the concepts that express it and to the echo it finds in a given moment of history. But "the text without the *Spirit* is nothing" (Angelus Silesius). To desire to seek out the "sense" of the text solely in the text is to forget that the text's truth is discovered beyond its expression. The sense is not a prisoner of the text; it is not "a ready-made meaning," because according to linguists and philosophers, the sense is open and points forward. "The meaning of books lies ahead of them" (Gérard Genette); their sense is "a sense which orients" (Emmanuel Lévinas). This is what contemporary authors are trying to remind us of when they take up the formula of John Scotus Erigena: "The interpretation of Sacred Scripture is infinite."[51]

As we can see, what is at stake here is a philosophical question: What does it mean to interpret Sacred Scripture? Where is the sense of the biblical

---

50. J.-M. Sevrin, "L'exégèse critique comme discipline théologique," in *RThL* 21 (1990): 146-62 (cf. p. 151).

51. See above, note 45.

text to be found? The answer to these questions does not have to do with exegetical method, but rather with that which Blondel called "the prolegomena to all future exegesis." In order to facilitate a better understanding of everything that is implied in the problem of exceeding the text, an excess that allows us truly to come to *comprehend* it, we think it useful to recall what we learned from recent philosophical hermeneutics: "to interpret," says Heidegger, alluding to the etymology of the German *Aus-legen* (which could be translated "to lay out," "ex-posit," Fr. "dé-ployer"), consists in "saying" the "unsaid" of things said. Kant already observed that this is the constant effort to "liberate and safeguard the interior forces" of the text, to let its hidden and inexhaustible dynamism be seen. Equally for Blondel, to interpret is to pass "from the implicit as 'enjoyed' into something explicit and known."[52] And Jean Guitton reminded us not long ago: "Beyond the words, there is the inexpressible meaning."[53] According to Pareyson, along the same lines, the relationship between truth and its formulations possesses a hermeneutic character; for this reason, "to comprehend means to interpret, to deepen what is explicit by grasping in it that infinite implicit which it heralds and contains."[54] This because in texts, as Ricoeur repeatedly tells us, there is always a "surplus of meaning." These repeated and convergent admonitions of modern philosophers seem to echo what the Fathers repeatedly said about the *mira profunditas* of Scripture. They especially remind us of various passages of St. Jerome, who distinguished in Scripture *superficies et medulla, folia et radix comprehensionis, verba et sensus, littera et spiritus.*[55] What is at stake, then, is a recovery of that which other Latin Fathers, especially St. Gregory, called the *interior intelligentia* of the texts of Scripture, the interior reality that is hidden in them[56] and the mystery of salvation history that is revealed there.

52. "History and Dogma," p. 268.

53. J. Guitton, *L'absurde et le mystère* (Paris: Desclée de Brouwer, 1984), p. 26.

54. L. Pareyson, *Verità e interpretazione* (Milan: Mursia, 1971), p. 22.

55. Cf. my study, "Interpretation of the Holy Scripture in the Spirit in Which It Was Written (Dei Verbum 12c)," pp. 223-33, where I cite various texts of the Fathers, especially Origen and St. Jerome.

56. See the noteworthy work of C. Dagens, *Saint Grégoire le Grand: Culture et experiences chrétiennes* (Paris: Études Augustiniennes, 1977), esp. ch. 3: "Gregory's Theory of Knowledge: The 'Interna Intelligentia'" (pp. 205-44). Cf. particularly pp. 233-37: "Gregory's Exegesis: The Exterior Sense and the Interior Sense."

It is the discovery of the spiritual sense of Scripture which, without ever doing violence to the letter, penetrates as far as the Spirit. This is what the Council wishes to communicate to us today when it asks us to interpret Sacred Scripture "in the sacred Spirit in which it was written."

c. How do we bring about this work of interpretation, that is, how do we arrive at a profound understanding of the sense of Scripture without falling into arbitrariness? We begin with the simplest recommendations of the gospels: "The words that I have spoken to you are spirit and life" (John 6:63).[57] In Jesus' *words*, we must seek their *spirit*, which is the spirit of Jesus, but also their profound *life*, which is the very life of Jesus.[58] The parable of the sower in the synoptic gospels also invites us to reflect: Jesus' word is not a stone, an inert object, but a seed (Mark 4:14; Luke 8:11), a seed of life. Once it falls into good soil, the grain of wheat first has to die (John 12:24), then it produces much fruit. For us to receive subjectively the "life" of the seed which is the Word of God, this seed has to have grown in the fertile soil of the People of God to which we belong, but it also has to grow *in us*, in our interiority. Conversely, from an objective standpoint, the text must be integrated into its broader context: first in the immediate context in which it was sown and sprouted, and then also in the later context in which it bore much fruit. The metaphor aside, this means that the text must be integrated both into the content and the unity of the whole Bible and in the living tradition of the whole Church (cf. DV 12). If the written text of the Word of God is truly life, it ultimately cannot be adequately understood except within the tradition of the Church, since it is precisely this tradition that is "the life of the Spirit in the Church" (Louis Bouyer). We must therefore be attentive to the *growth* of the Word, following the hermeneutical principle so dear to St. Gregory: "the divine words grow together with those who read them."[59] Along the same lines, Cardinal Ratzinger invites us to be sensitive to the "dynamism and depth of the

---

57. This text has been called "one of the most important biblical foundations of spiritual exegesis": D. Farkasfalvy, *L'inspiration de l'Écriture Sainte dans la théologie de Saint Bernard* (Rome: Herder, 1964), p. 96.

58. We recall in this regard the very suggestive text of Gottfried d'Admont cited above (pp. 38-39).

59. See p. 48 above.

Word,"[60] which means that we must "discover how each given historical word intrinsically transcends itself." Thus, we must acknowledge "the intrinsic rightness of the rereadings," precisely because these help make apparent all the interior wealth of the Word.[61] All this long process, this constant effort objectively to insert the texts into the whole Bible and the Tradition, must be accomplished by the subject — the reader and the interpreter of the Bible — within faith. In this regard, a norm for interpretation much used by the Fathers remains ever valid. It echoes a text from Isaiah (Isa 7:9, according to the Septuagint and the *Vetus Latina*): "If you do not believe, you will not be able to understand." Where Scripture is involved, believing is one of the conditions for understanding. It is from the initial faith that one comes, little by little, to a deeper comprehension: *gnosis*, in the sense given to it by the Fathers. This is the dynamic movement from *pistis* to *gnosis*, so well analyzed by Bouyer[62] and von Balthasar,[63] among others. As an illustration of this principle, we cite in conclusion two texts of Clement of Alexandria: "There is no knowledge without faith, and no faith without knowledge."[64] The adult Christian, the true "Gnostic," is he who has realized this whole program in himself: "*Faith*, but also the *knowledge* of the truth."[65]

Conclusion

This brings us back to our starting point. We said at the beginning that the study of the Bible, like the other ecclesiastical sciences, is threatened today by the secularization flooding our world. Those who dedicate themselves to

60. Above, p. 20.

61. Above, p. 26.

62. L. Bouyer, *Gnosis: La conaissance de Dieu dans l'Écriture* (Paris: Cerf, 1988).

63. H. Urs von Balthasar, *The Glory of the Lord: A Theological Aesthetics*, vol. 1: *Seeing the Form*, trans. Erasmo Leiva-Merikakis, ed. J. Fessio and J. Riches (Edinburgh/San Francisco: T. & T. Clark/Ignatius, 1983), chapter II A: "The Light of Faith" (pp. 131-218); cf. pp. 131-41: "Pistis and Gnosis."

64. Clement of Alexandria, *Stromata*, V.I.I.3 (SC 278, 24).

65. *Stromata*, II.II.52.3 (SC 38, 76).

scientific exegesis often ignore the tradition of the Church and believe that they must confine themselves to a series of purely technical operations outside of faith. But in doing this, they risk, in spite of their immense efforts, "always remaining in one place and learning, without ever arriving at the *knowledge of the truth*" (2 Tim 3:7). Why? Because the truth of Scripture is not truth in the positivistic sense of modern science, but rather "the grace of truth" (cf. John 1:14, 17), revealed truth, the gospel that saves us (cf. Eph 1:13). True scientific work that concerns itself with this truth cannot be practiced except within a "science of faith." This is what Bouyer reminded us of so opportunely in his last book, which we quote in conclusion:

> If a *science of the Bible* is possible, this cannot but be a particular and particularly fundamental form of the *science of theology*. This means that biblical science cannot but be a *science of faith*, since it cannot develop without contradiction outside of faith: that faith which the Bible takes upon itself to instill and nourish.[66]

Translated by Michelle Borras

---

66. L. Bouyer, *Gnosis*, p. 145; italics mine.

Is a Biblical Theology Possible?

Paul Beauchamp

The title of this contribution may be surprising. A friend saw me writing and invited me to change it: "Is a *non-biblical* theology possible?" — he suggested. I answered: "Blessed are you, who are not a theologian; as for me, I probably am, seeing that I ask such unexpected questions!" I therefore ought immediately to reassure the readers about my conviction: a biblical theology is possible. It is possible because it exists, but under different forms. As I go about describing them, I will, little by little, specify the meaning of my question.

It is for me a great joy to offer these simple reflections in honor of Cardinal Carlo Maria Martini: his pastoral activity is animated by the belief that the biblical message can reach the Christian people, indicating thus to exegetes, for their great encouragement, the roots and the source of biblical theology.

The Reality and the Wish

Biblical theology exists, but not by itself: it relies on the research done in all the textual and historical sciences. Having said this, it will be enough to recall that the encyclical *Divino Afflante Spiritu* (1943) established as the primary (*potissimum*) objective of exegesis the elucidation of the theological doctrine of the texts (EB 551), in order to make it understood that exegesis and theology should not be separated too much. It should be noted, however, that the (enthusiastic) reception of *Divino Afflante* perhaps did not match this emphasis of the encyclical with a coefficient as elevated as this *potissimum*. I would gladly propose registering the works that were more responsive to this call of the encyclical under the name of "theological exegesis."

It is true that today we are familiar with such current terms as "Deuteronomist theology," "theology of the Priestly author," "Johannine theology," and "Pauline theology." In the sphere of university publications, considerable esteem was obtained and merited by works such as the "Dictionaries of Biblical Theology," which have as their archetype the celebrated Kittel, or the didactic works of synthesis published under the name of "Theology of the Old Testament" or of the "New Testament," even if among this last group there is a smaller number of successful works.

But already here, there is an uncertainty, a problem. For the Old Testament, it is evident that we cannot identify *sic et simpliciter* a theology of the Old Testament with our theology: we cannot transform it into Christian theology!

For the New Testament, the didactic works entitled "Theologies of the New Testament" do not feel the obligation to give their opinion on the level of unity of the literature that they describe. They prefer rather to make it appear in its diversity, which is real, or even in its divergences. Science obliges us not to conceal them, and even to make them manifest to us, in the case that habit has rendered us insensitive to them.

In asking myself if a biblical theology is possible, I wonder if it is possible to have a theology that is not only Pauline, or Johannine, or of only one Testament. In any case, such a theology corresponds to a very deep reality. A biblical theology is called in the end to honor the right of this superior reality that we call "the Bible," which unites, in one book alone, two Testaments whose unity has been as radically affirmed by Christians as it has been contested by Jews. In short, I wonder above all if it is possible to have a theology that spans the two Testaments. This is my real question. Such a theology is what encounters greater obstacles, because it spans greater differences. Here would be the place to situate the transition from the sphere of theological exegesis in the direction of that of biblical theology, defining this last term as that which illustrates the relationship and the break between the two Testaments and discovers their principles. But the simple announcement of the project founded on the union of the two Testaments can give the impression of an illusory mirage. So, before proposing an answer, without a doubt it will be necessary also to declare with a certain detachment and without illusion: Who knows? The boldness of utopia can receive, in recompense, the grace of lightness. In any case, we will have to get rid of a lot of baggage in order to dare a crossing so wide, this going and coming from one Testament to the other! A crossing that I certainly have not yet completed! And, if then I should have completed it, I should have to undertake it again immediately, or rather, be glad that others undertake it again along other paths. "Forgive a little my madness," said St. Paul to the Corinthians (I would gladly adopt this motto!). With greater moderation, let us say that a theology that spans the two Testaments is the expression of a wish. It is the object intended by an impulse of the believing intelligence, which in a certain sense does not ask itself so much if its wish is effectively possible.

This wish has been expressed many times. Certainly I am not innovating by reformulating it.

In 1956, Fr. Roland de Vaux, with regard to a biblical theology "founded on the two Testaments," said that it is "*the last end* of our studies."[1] In 1960, G. von Rad saw a biblical theology capable of "overcoming the dualism" between "arbitrarily separated" treatments of the Old Testament and of the New Testament as "the yet very distant objective of our efforts." In 1964, Cardinal A. Bea, invited to write some pages in the great dictionary of Kittel,[2] saluted this work as "the most important achievement for the world of contemporary Protestant exegesis," but wished that one day the same author would be the one to treat "in the same spirit" every word of both testaments. In passing, he signaled "the undeniable drawback" of separating them in teaching. (To my knowledge, this wish has not been fulfilled.) In 1977, A. H. J. Gunneweg affirmed his own conviction: "It would be no exaggeration to understand the hermeneutical problem of the Old Testament as *the* problem of Christian theology, and not just as one

---

1. R. de Vaux, "A propos de la Théologie Biblique," in *ZAW* 68 (1956); 225-27, at 226.

2. G. Kittel and G. Friedrich, eds., *Theologisches Wörterbuch zum Neuen Testament*, I-X (Stuttgart: W. Kohlhammer, 1933-1979); English translation: *TDNT*.

problem among others."[3] For my part, in 1976, I presented my work *L'un et l'autre Testament*, vol. 1, with the subtitle: *Essay-Attempt at Reading*,[4] indeed just as Grelot in 1962 had presented his *Sens chrétien de l'Ancien Testament* as *Sketch of a Treatise*.[5] From this rapid panorama of the literature, let us hold onto two observations: "last intentionality" and "initial attempt." It is now time to make room for what motivates and strengthens the wish of which I have been speaking.

A Theology of the Two Testaments Is Necessary Today

What motivates the intention to aim at a theology of the two Testaments (which is the meaning I give now to the expression "biblical theology") is the feeling of its necessity, of its urgent necessity. The question of knowing whether it is possible becomes therefore secondary.

This motivation springs from current events, and will be considered under three aspects: relations between Christians and Jews, the relationship of the gospel to cultures, and Christian clarification with respect to contemporary violence.

Christian-Jewish Relations

I will mention, in the first place, the change in the relationship lived for centuries between Christianity and the Jewish people, a change periodically fed by the interventions of John Paul II which, in this sphere, turn things upside down. In university circles, this change involves three paths: the study of the tradition of the Judaism that still exists around us; the study of the

---

3. A. H. J. Gunneweg, *Vom Verstehen des Alten Testaments. Eine Hermeneutik* (Göttingen: Vandenhoeck & Ruprecht, 1977) (GAT 5), p. 7. English translation: *Understanding the Old Testament*, trans. John Bowden, OTL (Philadelphia: Westminster, 1978), p. 2.

4. P. Beauchamp, *L'un et l'autre Testament*, I. *Essai de lecture* (Paris: Éditions du Seuil, 1976).

5. P. Grelot, *Sens chrétien de l'Ancien Testament. Esquisse d'un traité dogmatique* (Tournai: Descleé, 1962).

synchronic relations between "the Jesus movement" (*Jesusbewegung*), on the one hand, and the Judaism of his time, on the other; and lastly (but more seldom) *the study of the fidelity of the same "Jesus movement" to the heritage of the First Testament,* since, at least in part, the reading done of it by Jesus and his disciples differs with respect to that done in the surrounding environment. I consider this third approach to be more specific to biblical theology.

In theological terms we can distinguish two phases. *The first:* Does the New Testament teach the fulfillment of the Scriptures as an essential datum of the faith? It is a level that we can call juridical or normative. The question of knowing whether Jesus truly believed it (A. Schweitzer thought so, and so do I) and whether he truly taught it himself is, from the theological point of view, subordinate. *The second:* How do we understand this teaching of the New Testament in such a way that we can give it our assent? "The act of Jesus fulfills the Scriptures of the Old Testament": by what lights are we brought to affirm such an understanding, and what lights do we receive from it?

At the same time, exciting and very fruitful is the search to see if the image of a suffering Messiah in the ancient prophecies has some connection to the Judaism contemporary to Jesus, whether only some small clue be found or whether none be found at all. I leave the question open. I cannot stop thinking, however, that in the modern era a much simpler question has been neglected: Could an upright man who read the Scriptures at the time of Jesus be led to find in them the image of a suffering savior, even if no one around him had seen him? And if so, by what path? We cannot answer if we do not ourselves attempt this reading at our own expense. The relationship between Jesus and his immediate contemporaries does not offer the key to the proper reading. There is room for the hypothesis of an innovative school of reading, founded by Jesus. It can simultaneously feed itself from the Jewish reading, and yet find itself radically different from it.

The Gospel and Cultures

I will make mention *in second place,* among the motivations for a theology of the two Testaments, our awareness of the need to establish a relationship between the proclamation of the gospel and cultures. The New Testament is the fruit of a culture, of which, however, it does not give a description: it is the product of a brief *moment* in history. The Old Testament, on the contrary, is one of the great *monuments* of the history of humanity that embraces many eras and many places, and also two languages in the Catholic or Orthodox canon. The gospel presents itself thus as the key to understand, as the way to love, judge, and save an entire cultural whole. The Bible does not put the gospel face to face with all cultures. But the hypothesis can be advanced that the relationship of the gospel to cultures — in the different memories of humanity — cannot be understood without a study of the prehistory of the gospel, which is precisely the First Testament. It is not the simple flowering of this past, since it provokes a terrible crisis on that same ground from which it rises, yet nevertheless, "he did not come to abolish." *In the relationship of the gospel to every culture, we cannot be spared the dimension of "crisis" in its most radical sense, a crisis for which the life of Jesus offers the definitive model.* But the crisis, in the measure itself in which it is radical — and if it is allowed to be radical — has an innovating effect on the glance toward, on the reading of *every* cultural heritage. If inspired by the relationship of the two Testaments, the glance turned to a culture's past is not only selective, engaged in making choices; rather, it renews texts and traditions with the breath of the Spirit, just as the glance of Jesus and his own on the tradition was innovative, finding there "treasures hidden since the foundation of the world." This glance discovered in the Old Testament a meaning and truths that no scientific procedure could discover.

Biblical Law and the Violence of the World

A *third* motivation is internal to the Church itself, in the face of the violence in the world. The more extensive, emphasized, and sensible presence of the Old Testament in the readings of our liturgy has strongly posed such a question. For the one who participates in it, the experience itself of being subjected by this reading to an authentic tension is a rough yet beneficial treatment. The whole Old Testament is conceived in such a way as to encourage the observance of the law of Moses: Christians who listen to its proclamation should be called on, sooner or later, to give an explanation as to why they do not need to observe it. Exegesis is not enough. I will not insist on this point.

The breaking points between the two economies do not stop here. Why is it that, during the Paschal night, we read as a work of God (joined to that of the "Exterminator") the massacre of the firstborn of Egypt? The preacher — assuming he dares to speak about it — will explain the matter as the trace of a still-primitive stage of humanity. But who will feel satisfied with this dull commentary, which theologians do not necessarily succeed in enriching, especially in our times when we have reason to challenge the idea that humankind has truly changed? Why then revive this memory, together with that of the passion of Jesus? This reading, nonetheless, will be necessary, having even an absolute necessity (a purged Old Testament is a detestable *impasse*, and a truly theological commentary would make itself the bearer of an irreplaceable light). The case of the wars of Israel demands completely special attention with regard to the fact that the same problem presents itself today to the conscience of Jews and Christians, both respectively illuminated by two millennia of such contrasting experiences, seeing that Christians, for their part, have for centuries brought again to life the wars of the Old Testament, while the Jews, in turn, were led by history to take up arms for a land again, up to a situation that still today has become among the most dramatic. There are numerous publications in the category of theological exegesis that deal with these problems: von Rad for Deuteronomy;[6] A. Neher for the theme of the conquest;[7] N. Lohfink for the Priestly tradition;[8] etc. Beyond theological exegesis, however, a biblical theology could be truly characterized as such on the condition of its making a path that goes from war all the way to the cross. We expect from a theology of the two Testaments that it know how again to mark out for us and in us that path that goes from universal violence to rec-

---

6. G. von Rad, *Der Heilige Krieg im alten Israel* (Zürich: Zwingli Verlag, 1951); English translation, *Holy War in Ancient Israel*, trans. and ed. M. J. Dawn (Grand Rapids: Eerdmans, 1991).

7. A. Neher, "Violence et non-violence: Israel et Canaan," in *Regards sur une tradition* (Paris: Bibliophane, 1989), pp. 168-85.

8. N. Lohfink, "Die Schichten des Pentateuch und der Krieg," in *Gewalt und Gewaltlosigkeit im Alten Testament* (Freiburg/Basel/Wien: Herder, 1983) (QD 96).

onciliation. A biblical theology cannot leave the ethical dimension on the side. The Bible invites us to find the place between idolatry and violence, between knowledge of God and peace on earth. The task is not necessarily undertaken only by theologians: a layman, R. Girard, has taken it on more than anyone else and has not withdrawn himself from the discussion with professional theologians.[9] With his successes and limits, recognized with *humor* by the same author, this example shows that biblical theology will be able to correspond to its proper definition only on the condition of its making room for anthropology as much as for knowledge of the book. More simply: *the knowledge of "man" should not be less than the knowledge of the book. With this condition, we will be able to speak of biblical theology.* Significantly, as vast as is the horizon embraced by Girard, his effective anthropological base consists of comparative literature, from Dostoevsky to Shakespeare, where he has found stimulus and impulse, beginning from a certain moment, for his biblical exploration. Aesthetics offers theology a line of departure. We will come back to this.

Jesus Christ and the Two Testaments

I have spoken about questions that demand a response because they are current issues. . . . The question of violence is always current. It is time, however, to make room for a broader point of view, namely, the witness given by the Old Testament to what Christian faith confesses regarding the identity of Jesus.

The Challenge

Jesus is the Christ, he is the Son of God, he is the eternal Word. On this theme, which summarizes the whole of theology, biblical theology is called to give its opinion, extending itself even to an innovative reading of the Old

9. R. Girard, *Quand ces choses commenceront . . . : Entretiens avec Michel Treguer* (Paris: Arléa, 1994) (a comprehensive and personal summary by the author).

Testament. If two independent witnesses, separated by time, see the same thing, according to what the assumed position allows them, then their testimony will have much more value and force. Precisely for this reason the task that summons the Old Testament to witness to Jesus Christ is a constitutive part of Christian theology. About this, the continuity of the tradition persuades us. This tradition is rooted in the New Testament. The Fourth Gospel gives us the most solemn and emphatic formulations, putting them in the mouth of Jesus, who says, with regard to Moses: "he wrote about me" (John 5:46). Or again: "Abraham saw my day" (cf. John 8:56). And, in the mouth of a disciple: "We have found him about whom Moses in the Law and the prophets wrote, Jesus . . ." (John 1:45). These affirmations, and many other similar ones, are a challenge to theology insofar as it is a methodical and rational procedure. Can we adopt them as hypotheses capable of giving an impulse to an exploration of the Old Testament? We have the right to ask: Why, in fact, are they not? Is a theology possible that does not assume them as a point of departure? Truly, the obstacle is noteworthy, and cannot be overcome without speculative resources that, habitually, are not required of exegesis.

Effectively, will a rational spirit be able to sustain that Moses truly wrote *about the subject* Jesus? It is indeed the case to say "subject," since the same subject Jesus gives his own person as the referent of the writings of Moses. Certainly, John lends these words to the "subject" Jesus under the action of the Spirit who "guides him into all the truth" (John 16:13); the theologian adheres to this revelation. Some could even admit that Moses wrote about a messiah in the sense that he set down the general concept, and Jesus came one day to correspond precisely to that concept (Jesus *"casus in casibus,"* says Kierkegaard with a satirical tone), so that Jesus would have come to satisfy a pre-established definition. Now, though not excluding this, the Gospel of John goes much further: Moses wrote about a messiah who is none other than the one who says "I," reaching him in his singularity and individuality. It is, to tell the truth, the indispensable condition in order that Jesus be recognized as son of God by nature, qualified by the "Name above every other name." Precisely here the challenge and the light are intensified. The act of writing done by Moses and the person of Jesus thus find themselves in a proximity as close as the interior glance of Abraham and the same irreplaceable identity of Jesus. The intentions of the Johannine narrative already rise up to the height of those who recognize in the flesh of Jesus of Nazareth the flesh of the eternal Word. They are there to suggest to us by what way the Johannine prologue or the highest affirmations of the Pauline captivity letters were possible and necessary: it was not possible to say that Jesus was the Word and that "the Word was God" without passing through an innovative reading of the Old Testament of which the New Testament offers multiple examples.

The Commitment of the Subject-Reader

Here, we are dealing with a postulate of faith, on the basis of which the research is called to advance a hypothesis. This hypothesis will have to be verified by the researcher, who is subjected to the obligation of exposing himself to criticism, and therefore of putting himself at the school of modern (pre-modern?) exegesis, born in the twentieth century — whether dealing with theological exegesis or also with purely historical exegesis. But if he wants to do the work of biblical theology, nothing can dispense him from committing himself at his expense — as I have just recalled — to the path of an innovative reading of the Old Testament, something that the exegesis born in the nineteenth century precisely does not teach. Such a reading will be innovative not only in relation to this objective reading of science, *but it will also be so in relation to that reading of the Old Testament proposed by the New Testament itself.* Let me explain. Evidently, the New Testament is our norm. As regards principles, it is evident that it offers us the points of reference of the path. But everyone knows that all of its arguments on the harmony of the two Testaments cannot today be adopted as one block. Frequently it happens that one is able to share only in its basic conviction, namely: when he was "still with them," still before his resurrection, Jesus initiated his own into a new understanding of the Scriptures (Luke 24:44), which in our turn we have to rediscover, according to what Jesus effectively is.

The reason for this is simple, or, at least, we can propose the principal one, which emerges as from an immense mass and dominates it: Jesus, in the unicity of his person, professes that the ancient Scriptures speak about him as about a unique subject — which signifies, naturally: not as a person different from another, but inasmuch as this "common" difference is assumed and transcended in virtue of his divine filiation. This truth known by faith cannot be perceived except by a subject-reader so committed. This is not only because it is truth communicated through the faith accorded to a revelation, but also because this last assumes and transcends such a kind of communication possible only between freedoms.

We thus discover two openings. On the one hand, we understand how the task of a Christian theology of the two Testaments remains properly inaccessible to a pure and solitary science, and is not obtainable from what can be demonstrated with the sole power of reason by way of conclusion of historical research. On the other hand, from the point of view of the history of Christian doctrine, we understand why, up to a relatively recent period (let us say approximately corresponding to the Second Vatican Council), the Christian theology of the two Testaments, though wished for by more than one voice, encountered obstacles in the modern (or premodern?) era.

The Course of the Research

I would like now to take up again these two aspects: the loci of freedom and its obstacles. It is not enough to say that the theology of the two Testaments takes upon itself a revealed proposition that is directed to the faith. Being free and freeing, this faith will assume the course of those procedures of the spirit corresponding to its own sovereign freedom.

Ethics and Aesthetics

This freedom finds confirmation in many ways: in the sphere (already mentioned) of ethics and under the aesthetic form of the narrative.

It is exercised and confirmed in the measure in which it responds to the imperatives of *ethics*. Now, the Bible itself connects access to knowledge with purity of heart. A tradition that dates to Isaiah (ch. 6), taken up by Pascal, sees in the obscurity of the parables an effect of the resistance of the heart rendered obtuse by sin. Already, the disciples of Emmaus were accused of being "foolish and slow of heart" (Luke 24:25). The opacity of the Scriptures has repeatedly been placed alongside the opacity of the parables. We recover here, by a rather underground but precise way, what I just said regarding the mystery of the violence of the biblical wars, violence converted in the cross of Christ. It is not at all evident how this mystery can be illuminated by a gnosis that would draw out its own proper knowledge, separating it from the conversion in progress.

The same sovereign freedom is exercised and confirmed in the sphere of *aesthetics*. Every work of art has the profile of a demonstration of freedom, which is valid also for its reader, whether or not we are dealing with that commentator called an "art critic." And everyone knows that this freedom is reinforced by strict requirements, obeying rules no less imperious than the rules of a game. The innovative reading of the Old Testament is related to poetics, which finds support not only in the importance of texts written in verse (such as prophecies, psalms, the Canticle). No theology of the two Testaments will be possible today without a theory of narrative, not only oriented toward a current practice of analysis, but founded on a philosophy of the narrative act — an enterprise in which the work of Paul Ricoeur stands out.[10]

Every narrative gives back a series of acts of freedom, presumes an imaginative (therefore aesthetic) participation of the reader in the wish of the "actants" (or characters) according to the figures that cross his path, and directs itself to the freedom of a receiver for the purpose of conferring upon his decision a charge of energy necessary for his own praxis. Upon these characteristics is founded the articulation of the aesthetic and the ethical. A theology of the two Testaments is called to have recourse to a science of forms and of their rules (not formulated!) that would allow it to classify the different types of narrative, their function, and their realization

---

10. We point out a thesis recently published at Louvain, which comments on this work, insisting on its applications to the biblical sphere, possible or already available: A. Thomasset, *Paul Ricoeur, une poétique de la morale: Aux fondements d'une éthique, herméneutique et narrative dans une perspective chrétienne* (Leuven: University Press, 1996) (BEThL 124).

in relation to the ultimate narrative that is the life of Jesus, the figure *par excellence* within whom our decisions take impulse. Referred and expanded to the first narratives in the First Testament, to the prototypical narratives of the Pentateuch, the biblical narrative will find its impulse still more pronounced; it will make us experience the mystery of its elusive origin, back even to the "bosom of the Father" of which the Johannine prologue speaks. The same research will also have to situate the narrative in relation to other modes of expression, in first place to the law. In going back to the inaccessible origin, our reading of the biblical narrative will encounter its end: at the same time and in conflict, the law and the cross. It is not necessary that the narrative tell us everything; in fact, it is rather necessary that it not tell us everything. The longer the crossing of the ocean, the more daring the climb, the more economical also will the selected itinerary have to be. Constitutive of the freedom of this enterprise is the fact of not imposing itself on anyone, but of eliciting other enterprises that are different. Is it not the case that the Bible itself does not cease to elicit in us a discourse that is not its own?

Obstacles

I have just said that to outline this perspective means simultaneously to say why it has found obstacles. Now is not the time to detain ourselves too much considering it. But a scruple of accuracy obliges me at least to underline that we are dealing with obstacles that are found every time a change of level happens. For a long time, discourse on the Bible looked for a type of certainty that is not at all what we are proposing — it will be necessary yet to say it — by way of conclusion. The modern or pre-modern era had exempted itself from the obligation of reading the Bible starting from the certainties of the faith. The Church, which remained faithful to these same certainties, opened an era of transition, during which it has above all asked exegetes to find those certainties that all human beings can share: those of historical exactitude. Even theological exegesis was invited to distance itself very little from the level of description and from the history of ideas. The current moment is an invitation to a biblical theology that proceeds according to an alliance of the aesthetic and the ethical. Thanks to this alliance, it will involve a discourse that is at the same time directed to every person and oriented by the wish to propose to him, according to the occasion and with respect, "the thing itself." One freedom offers itself to another freedom.

Conclusion

It seems that I still hear our teachers, when they imparted sobriety to us as the principal quality of exegesis, *nüchtern*. At times it was difficult for us even just to drink at will. It seems that I hear, for example, Karl Barth. Even though I never met him, the following lines from a preface to his commentary on Romans "speak to me": his procedure in the commentary on the text is — he says — that of being "driven on till I stand with [virtually] nothing before me but the enigma of the [object]...."[11] In this "virtually" [*nahezu*] or in this "nothing but" [*nur*], the distance to maintain will be rather variable depending on each one, as also depending on the moments of each one.... Karl Barth adds, for his part, that this intention will merit that he be "severely handled," but — he says — "it is stronger than I am." One will conclude that he is therefore more a theologian than an exegete, but the exegesis will gain for us always to advance toward what Barth calls that "object," which is not at all an enemy of the "subject" mentioned above, since their encounter is what I earlier called "the thing itself."

Translated by Pablo Gadenz

11. K. Barth, *Der Römerbrief* (München: Chr. Kaiser, ²1921), p. xi; English translation, *The Epistle to the Romans*, trans. E. C. Hoskyns (London: Oxford University Press, 1933), p. 8. The quote is from the Preface to the Second Edition.

Exegesis: Reading the Scriptures in Faith

Bruna Costacurta

The horizon of the biblical exegete who studies and interprets the sacred text cannot but be that of a "believer" working in faith. Sacred Scripture appears with a wholly particular status: it is both human and divine word. In it, the eternal Word of God takes on flesh in the words of human authors.

In the biblical text, a reality of revelation and of the particular presence of God is at work, making this text different from every other. It claims to be an ultimate word pronounced on reality, revealing its meaning and its deepest truth. For this reason, one cannot approach it without acknowledging and respecting its peculiar characteristics. On the other hand, only faith is capable of discerning and receiving these in all their consequences.

It is well known that contemporary exegesis is raising questions about its path, especially regarding its status as a science and the various methods it employs.[1] The great debate appears to be between the historical-critical,

---

1. Cf. J. Barton, *Reading the Old Testament: Method in Biblical Study* (London: Longman & Todd, ²1996); L. Alonso-Schökel, "Of Methods and Models," in J. A. Emerton, ed., *Congress Volume: Salamanca, 1983* (VTS, 36) (Leiden: Brill, 1985), pp. 3-13; "Trends: Plurality of Methods, Priority of Issues," in J. A. Emerton, ed., *Congress Volume: Jerusalem, 1986* (VTS, 40) (Leiden: Brill, 1988), pp. 285-97; F. Raurell, "Lettura plurale del testo: Metodi biblici," *Laur* 29 (1988): 251-86; R. Rendtorff, "Between Historical Criticism and Holistic Interpretation: New Trends in Old Testament Exegesis," in J. A. Emerton,

or diachronic, method and other "holistic" and synchronic methods. Beyond the various methodological choices, however, the real problem lies in the hermeneutical attitude that accompanies them and the interpretative finality they must serve. Once the assumption has been made that exegesis has to be scientific, the question arises to which notion of science one ought to refer, and what the preconceptions are that condition it. In the end, the question is this: Ought and can the interpretation of the sacred text be theological, explicitly open to the demands of faith in an awareness of its own ecclesial function?[2]

If Scripture is accepted in its truth as an inspired book, it seems that in order to understand it, we cannot limit ourselves to a study that is merely historical, linguistic, literary, structural, etc., but rather, keeping in mind the results of all these approaches, we must discover its properly religious sense. It is the religious and spiritual message that must be sought, and it is this message that becomes normative for the man of every age who places himself in an attitude of listening to the Word.

This obviously does not mean that we fall into pietism or fundamentalism, nor that we place ourselves on the level of a naïve and pre-scientific reading of the biblical text. Some acquisitions of the historical-critical method have by now become the common property of scholars, especially an awareness of the long and complex process of formation that resulted in the biblical texts, the traces of which they bear.

Thus, what is involved is not ignoring the gradual evolution of the text and the problems connected to this: textual and philological difficulties,

---

ed., *Congress Volume: Jerusalem, 1986*, pp. 298-303; C. Conroy, "Riflessioni metodologiche su recenti studi della pericope di Naaman (2 Re 5)," in G. Marconi and G. Collins, eds., *Luca—Atti. Studi in onore di P. Emilio Rasco nel suo 70° compleanno* (Assisi: Cittadella, 1991), pp. 46-71.

2. In this sense is significant the publication entitled *L'esegesi cristiana oggi* (Casale Monferrato: Piemme, [3]2000 [orig. 1991]), in which some relevant scholars reflect about the "Christian" physiognomy exegesis must have in order to fulfill its interpretative ecclesial task referred to in both Testaments. In I. de la Potterie's contribution (published also in the present volume), exegesis is defined as a "science of faith." The choice of terms is important because it makes a claim for the scientific status of exegesis, but as a theological science in which faith is a constitutive element. See also A. Vanhoye, "Esegesi biblica e teologia: La questione dei metodi," *Sem* 31 (1991): 267-78.

techniques of composition, literary genres, historical context, etc.[3] To the contrary, all of this has to be placed at the service of interpretation, but in the explicit awareness that Scripture is a book of faith, written in faith and received in faith by the community of believers as normative for their life as believers.

This is, after all, the first "scientific" postulate for a correct relationship with a written text: to know what it is and that for which it was composed, then to respect this nature and intentionality through an investigative method that corresponds to it.[4]

In fact, this is the normal and even the spontaneous method with which one normally places oneself before a text. It would never occur to anyone to read one of La Fontaine's fables as if it were a zoological treatise on the behavior of animals. In the same way, one cannot read a text of faith as if it were merely a piece of ancient literature, on equal footing with those of so many other, similar cultures. Nor, conversely, can the text be engaged only in its dimension of divine revelation without an awareness of the fact that this latter is mediated through a literary composition.

The difficult task of biblical exegesis, called as it is to travel unique interpretative paths, is that of remaining faithful to the absolute and unrepeatable particularity of Scripture as an inspired book.

This hermeneutical decision draws several fundamental consequences in its wake. First of all, the object of analysis and study should be the *current state of the text*, in its last redaction. It is the final canonical form of

---

3. "The capacity of working on differentiated levels of research, using different methods and entering into scientific dialogue with various related disciplines . . . is something that ought to be considered normal for every exegete today": C. Conroy, "Riflessioni metodologiche," p. 70. Cf. also J. Barr, *Does Biblical Study Still Belong to Theology? An Inaugural Lecture Delivered before the University of Oxford on 26 May 1977* (Oxford: Clarendon, 1978), esp. pp. 15-16; M. G. Brett, *Biblical Criticism in Crisis? The Impact of the Canonical Approach on Old Testament Studies* (Cambridge: Cambridge University Press, 1991).

4. Cf. R. Guardini's epistemological principle, taken up again by I. de la Potterie in his article in the present volume: "no object of research can be understood well except by a mode of understanding adequate to its object" (above, p. 35). It is also common knowledge that, if a discourse is to be understood properly, it must be engaged within its specific "linguistic play" (according to Wittgenstein's terminology): cf. C. Huber, *Critica del sapere* (Rome: Gregorian University Press, 1989), pp. 208-22.

biblical writings that is normative for the faith of believers, and not the reconstruction of a hypothetical original text. Along these lines, the movement toward a "canonical approach," represented above all by Childs,[5] Sanders,[6] Rendtorff,[7] and others,[8] appears to be particularly significant.

Seeking the original form of a biblical passage and tracing the stages of its formation is certainly useful for understanding how the passage has come to be what it is. But beyond the numerous difficulties and the impression of arbitrariness that sometimes accompany such endeavors, which often yield merely hypothetical and not very convincing results,[9] we must still reflect on a problem that is, in my opinion, central. That is, the text reconstructed by literary criticism is in fact *not* the biblical text but something else, a new text that has been judged more authentic, more coherent,

---

5. Cf. B. S. Childs, *Biblical Theology in Crisis* (Philadelphia: Westminster, 1970); *Introduction to the Old Testament as Scripture* (Philadelphia: Fortress, 1979); *Old Testament Theology in a Canonical Context* (Philadelphia: Fortress, 1986). On the work of Childs, see also M. G. Brett, *Biblical Criticism in Crisis? The Impact of the Canonical Approach on Old Testament Studies* (Cambridge: Cambridge University Press, 1991).

6. Cf. A. Sanders, *Torah and Canon* (Philadelphia: Fortress, 1972); "Text and Canon: Old Testament and New," in P. Casetti, O. Keel, and A. Schenker, eds., *Mélanges Dominique Barthélemy. Études Bibliques offertes à l'occasion de son 60ᵉ anniversaire* (OBO 38) (Fribourg: Éditions Universitaires, 1981), pp. 373-94; *Canon and Community: A Guide to Canonical Criticism* (Philadelphia: Fortress, 1984); *From Sacred Story to Sacred Text: Canon as Paradigm* (Philadelphia: Fortress, 1987), pp. 195-200, "Select Bibliography in Canonical Criticism."

7. Cf. R. Rendtorff, "Between Historical Criticism and Holistic Interpretation."

8. Interest in the final form of the text is not a prerogative exclusively of the canonical approach, but also, for example, of literary/narrative, structural, and rhetorical analysis. However, it seems to me important to highlight the canonical approach in our context, for its explicit reference to faith, the believing community, and the theological form of the text. On the relations and confrontations between the various methods, cf. B. S. Childs, *Introduction to the Old Testament*, pp. 74-75; R. F. Melugin, "Canon and Exegetical Method," in G. M. Tucker, ed., *Canon, Theology and Old Testament Interpretation: Essays in Honor of B. S. Childs* (Philadelphia: Fortress, 1988), p. 51; R. Rendtorff, "Between Historical Criticism and Holistic Interpretation," pp. 300-303; J. Barton, *Reading the Old Testament: Method in Biblical Study* (Louisville: Westminster/John Knox, 1984), pp. 141-45 and 151-54.

9. Cf. A. Vanhoye, "Esegesi biblica e teologia," pp. 270-72. See also in the present volume the ample contribution of J. Ratzinger, "Biblical Interpretation in Conflict: On the Foundations and the Itinerary of Exegesis Today."

stylistically superior, or at any rate preferable because it corresponds better to certain pre-determined criteria.

Now, to study such a text, to make of it the object of interpretation, appears to lead us away from properly "biblical" exegesis (that is, exegesis of the Bible), because the Bible is what the canon defines and offers to us as a book of faith.

A synchronic reading of the final text, though without ignoring its formative stages, seems to be postulated by the normative character traditionally attributed to canonical texts.

In this regard, I would like to pause for a moment on a small example — no more than a detail. It has to do with a text, the final form of which presents difficulties that appear to demand a more coherent reconstruction, for the sake of eliminating oddities and discrepancies.

I refer to the famous narrative of Genesis 2 and 3 about the garden and the forbidden fruit. The narration presents us with a problem of internal contradiction, since in the initial description of the garden, two trees are mentioned: the tree of life at the center of the garden and the tree of the knowledge of good and evil (cf. Gen 2:9). Then, however, we hear nothing more of the tree of life until the end of chapter 3 (vv. 22-24), while the tree of the knowledge of good and evil is named in God's prohibition (2:17). In the rest of the story, it is this tree that is referred to as forbidden.

The problem arises because of the disappearance of the tree of life. It is accentuated by the fact that, at the moment of the temptation in Genesis 3, the woman, answering the serpent's question, says that God commanded them not to eat the fruit of the tree that is at the center of the garden (3:3). But initially, this was the description of the tree of life, not of the tree that is later forbidden. So is there one tree, or are there two? How do we explain the incongruity in the woman's answer?

Usually, commentators take for granted that she is speaking of the tree of the knowledge of good and evil, and they turn to explanations from various sources referring to the history of the tradition.[10] The problem is re-

---

10. Cf. for example G. von Rad, *Genesis: A Commentary* (London: SCM Press, ³1972), p. 78: "The suspicion can scarcely be suppressed that the duality of trees in the midst of the garden is only the result of a subsequent combination of two traditions."

solved by affirming that the narrative really only is concerned with one tree, which was prohibited and stood at the center of the garden; the motif of the tree of life was a later addition. Since the latter motif was secondary, it is brushed aside by the interpretation; this could also explain the subsequent designation of the other tree as the tree of the knowledge of good and evil.[11]

However, if we accept the text in the form in which the last (inspired) redactor willed it and as we have it today, then precisely the presence of the two trees becomes important for a spiritual understanding of the meaning of man. This is because the text would be saying that the human being cannot assimilate a global understanding of reality, that is, of good and evil, which is the prerogative of God alone, but he does have free access to life. The tree of life is his, as long as man accepts eating from it in a radical dependence on the Creator, and accepts his own truth as a creature by not eating of the tree of knowledge.

When the woman then answers the serpent, referring to the forbidden tree as if it were the tree of life, something is revealed of the typical confusion of the temptation to sin. It is as if, for the woman, the two trees had gotten confused, such that she was led to believe that life is impossible if one must accept the limits proper to the creature. Under the pressure of temptation, the command not to eat of the tree of the knowledge of good and evil, the offer and the condition of true life for man, becomes a command of death. The truth is confused in the woman's conscience, and so the path is opened for the decisive attack of the serpent.

This is only a small example, but one that can prompt us to face themes and texts that are much more complicated and important.

The hermeneutic decision that leads us to accept the canonical text as normative requires a second position: precisely because it has been established by a canon, Sacred Scripture must be accepted in its *totality* and as a *unity*.[12] The interpretation of the texts requires their insertion into the

11. Cf. C. Westermann, *Genesis 1–11* (Minneapolis: Augsburg, 1984), pp. 211-14 (with an ample bibliography).

12. Cf. J. Ratzinger, "Biblical Interpretation in Conflict," p. 6 above: "The fundamental presupposition on which theological understanding of the Bible rests is the unity of Scripture; the method that corresponds to this presupposition is that of the *analogia fidei*, that is,

global context of Scripture, because it is only in the completeness of Scripture that God's revelation is unfolded to man.

We must, therefore, accept the totality in a broad and unitary vision, in which not only the individual passages are important, but also the relations between them and, especially, the broader relationship between the Old and the New Testaments.[13] If the New Testament is the interpretation and fulfillment of the Old, it cannot be understood except in reference to that which it rereads and completes. Conversely, the Old Testament needs the New to attain a full understanding of its ultimate and deepest meaning.

Such a hermeneutical attitude, which is the attitude of the Church's tradition and to which authors such as Beauchamp gave decisive contributions,[14] leads us to the possibility of a synchronic reading, in the light of a Paschal faith. In this light, even the contradictions or discrepancies that seem at times to emerge between various texts of the Old and New Testaments become a source of richer interpretation, even in their problematic nature.

We think, for example, of the apparent contrast between the idea of God as judge and God as merciful, between the condemnation of sin and forgiveness, between the proclamation of the necessity for the guilty person alone to die and the definitive proclamation of an innocent man who dies for all. The most frequent temptation is that of suppressing the contradictory elements by holding only to one extreme and eliminating the other as secondary, non-original, belonging to other sources, or — as in the case of the Old and New Testaments — as the result of an evolution that ratifies the radical overcoming, that is, the nullification, of what came before.

---

the understanding of individual texts in light of the whole." Cf. the section entitled "The Unity of the Whole of Scripture" in I. de la Potterie's article in the present volume (pp. 48-51).

13. On the problem of the theological relationship between the Old and the New Testaments, cf. J. Barr, *Old and New in Interpretation: A Study of the Two Testaments* (London: SCM, 1966); D. L. Baker, *Two Testaments, One Bible: A Study of Some Modern Solutions to the Theological Problem of the Relationship between the Old and New Testament* (Leicester: InterVarsity, 1976).

14. See specially P. Beauchamp, *L'un et l'autre Testament, Tome II: Accomplir les Écritures* (Paris: Éditions du Seuil, 1990).

In fact, it is precisely in the simultaneous acceptance of the two poles of the contradiction that the intelligence of faith comes into play. Thus, we will have to understand how there cannot be real mercy without truth and therefore without justice, how only the accusation can open the one who has been accused to an awareness of his sin and therefore to forgiveness. And we will have to understand how the mystery of the Cross does not change the problem of condemnation and punishment, but rather of guilt, rendering innocent those who acknowledge themselves to be guilty.

We find ourselves face to face with enormous issues, which we do not have the time even to touch on briefly. It seems important to me, however, to stress in my conclusion that, a little like the two trees of Genesis, it is not through simplification that we arrive at the fullest meaning of biblical revelation.

At bottom, the contradiction is part of faith and must be received in faith, in the light of the ultimate and definitive paradox that Festus so succinctly describes to Agrippa: they are questions "about one Jesus, who was dead, but whom Paul asserted to be alive" (Acts 25:19).

Translated by Michelle Borras

Christ in Contemporary Exegesis:
Where We Are and Where We Are Going

KLEMENS STOCK

This topic is vast and complex,[1] and we can deal only with this or that selected aspect. In what follows, "Christ" is not understood in a narrow sense as referring merely to a post-Paschal interpretation of Jesus. Rather, it stands for the figure of Jesus of Nazareth as a whole.

Outline of the Situation Today

We present our outline in five theses, chosen somewhat at random.

THESIS 1: The gap between the pre-Paschal Jesus and the post-Paschal Christ has shrunk somewhat.

Up until the middle of the last century, the pre-Paschal Jesus and the post-Paschal Christ were seen as sharply opposed. The former was the earthly Jesus who had proclaimed the kingdom of God. The latter had, after Easter, become the content of proclamation — Christ, Son of God, Re-

---

1. See W. G. Kümmel's 706-page bibliographical survey, *Vierzig Jahre Jesusforschung (1950-1990)* (BBB 91) (Weinheim: Beltz Athenäum, 1994). For a more recent *status quaestionis*: J. Roloff, *Jesusforschung am Ausgang des 20. Jahrhunderts* (SBAW.PH, 1998/4) (München: Verlag der Bayerischen Akademie der Wissenschaften, 1998).

deemer. The two were separated by a deep chasm, and there was nary a bridge between them.

Scholarship at this stage was evaluated in very different ways. I cite just two — extreme — positions. According to Rudolf Bultmann (†1976), the pre-Paschal Jesus is irrelevant to faith. He, like the early Church, is part of the history of Judaism. Christ, the Son of God, is a myth created by the Hellenistic community, especially by Paul, as an attractive cultic hero who could compete on the market of ancient mystery religions. This post-Paschal Christ has to be demythologized. All that counts is the word of the Cross: "that I am a sinner and that God forgives my sins in Christ." We must accept this word in faith. Faith has no doctrinal content; it is nothing other than voluntary, total self-surrender to God.

According to Joachim Jeremias (†1979), by contrast, everything hinges on the pre-Paschal, earthly Jesus discovered by historical-critical scholarship. It is in him, during his lifetime, that revelation occurred. What he actually said and did, how he actually interpreted his own person and work, so far as that can be ascertained, is binding. Everything else is dubious. The gospels already contain post-Paschal interpretation. The scholar's task, then, is to separate what comes from Jesus himself as clearly as possible from this interpretation. Only this genuine legacy of Jesus secures the solid ground we are seeking. As Heinrich Schlier (†1978) puts it, Jeremias makes "the historical Jesus nothing less than a fifth gospel and the criterion of the four gospels."

Bridges have now begun to appear over the gulf, and we owe them precisely to the scholarly research of Jeremias and others into the historical Jesus. This research has brought to light, for example, the so-called "implicit Christology" of the gospels. The words and deeds of the historical Jesus manifest an extraordinary and unique claim and self-understanding. This discovery has relativized things like the question of which titles ("explicit Christology") the earthly Jesus did or did not apply to himself. His claim and his self-understanding show up in a more real, more historically tangible way in his words and deeds than in his titles. Pre-Paschal implicit Christology provides a firm foundation for post-Paschal explicit Christology. The latter does not invent, does not overlay with arbitrary interpretations. It declares explicitly, proclaims, and confesses what is already contained in the person and work of the pre-Paschal Jesus.

THESIS 2: The search for the "historical Jesus" continues.

This claim requires no further proof. It suffices to refer the reader to Werner Georg Kümmel's account of the present state of the scholarship.[2] The topics are innumerable. Old issues can continually reemerge, because the limited state of the sources rules out any definitive answer to many questions. In the last fifteen years another stage has crystallized, known already as the "Third Quest," which proposes novel views regarding the history of Jesus.[3] In this context, the sociological approach to the gospels has assumed particular importance.[4] All of these investigations have their importance. Jesus, after all, was a historical personality, so that it is always possible to investigate him historico-critically from a wide variety of angles. This investigation is of basic importance for fundamental theology. But there needs to be an awareness that the issues involved are not all equally important. There needs to be a clear realization that the whole of exegesis cannot be reduced to the question about the "historical Jesus."

THESIS 3: There is a growing distance from historical-critical exegesis from many sides.

The phenomena I am about to list are quite heterogeneous. The one thing they do have in common is a dissatisfaction with historical-critical exegesis — a dissatisfaction that has different motives in each case.

a. Historical-critical exegesis is reproached for offering only hypotheses, and not bread that people can live on. During the 1960s, there was a great desire to catch up with the discoveries of modern exegesis. There was an eager attempt to popularize the works of the exegetes in theological and

2. See note 1.

3. B. Witherington III, *The Jesus Quest: The Third Search for the Jew of Nazareth* (Downers Grove, IL: InterVarsity, 1995). See J. P. Meier, "The Present State of the 'Third Quest' for the Historical Jesus: Loss and Gain," in *Bib* 80 (1999): 459-87. Its most controversial expression is the group known as the "Jesus Seminar," headed by J. D. Crossan and R. W. Funk.

4. See G. Theissen and A. Merz, *The Historical Jesus: A Comprehensive Guide* (London: SCM Press, 1998 [original: 1996]); B. J. Malina, *The Social Gospel of Jesus: The Kingdom of God in Mediterranean Perspective* (Minneapolis: Fortress, 2001).

catechetical formation, religious books, Bible studies, and lectures on biblical subjects. This eagerness has abated, and has given way to a certain lack
of enthusiasm, or even disappointment, towards the Bible. However much
one knows about the Bible, one can't live, that is, live as a believer, on things
like the ascertainment of literary form, the comparison between the Synoptics, or the distinction of sources. Historical-critical exegesis, with its
roster of issues, is predominantly absorbed with questions like these: Who
did or said what when, under what circumstances, and in what order? Interest in content and meaning becomes secondary. What the text is trying
to say is neglected. This has led to a call for a greater consideration of *the
message of Scripture*.

b. From another angle, the historical-critical method is reproached for
its disconnection from praxis. Its hypotheses and findings can be stored in
libraries. They can feed self-absorbed scholarship, but they cannot be put
into practice. Such exegesis turns Jesus, it is said, into an object of scholarship, and so is prevented from serving as a model and a stimulus to practical action. Fernando Belo (to take one example) attempts to remedy this
situation with his materialistic interpretation of the Gospel of Mark.[5] According to him, what characterized Jesus was his *powerful messianic praxis*,
which led him to fight for the poor and disadvantaged against the ruling
classes of his day. This struggle claimed his life. But the narration of his
deeds remains an important tool for the class struggle. It serves to make
the poor aware of their task and to propagate revolution. What is said in
the gospel about Jesus' relation to God, the saving meaning of his death,
and so forth, Belo considers to be a later theological-ideological re-
elaboration. It is along these same lines that one must locate "feminist"
exegesis, developed widely in the past several years and originated in a "liberationist" interpretation of the Bible; its intention is to "re-imagine Jesus'
actions according to a feminist reading."[6] It is difficult to shun the impression left by these approaches, both the liberationist and the feminist,

5. F. Belo, *A Materialist Reading of the Gospel of Mark* (Maryknoll, NY: Orbis Books,
1981 [original: 1975]).

6. E. Schüssler Fiorenza, *Jesus, Myriam's Child, Sophia's Prophet: Critical Issues in Feminist Theology* (London: SCM Press, 1995), back cover.

whereby they tend to project upon the gospel texts socio-political categories that are foreign to them.

c. Another approach to recovering the significance of the gospel and of Jesus for illuminating and sustaining believers' lives has been to *interpret them according to the categories of depth psychology.*[7] So far, this approach has not produced an abundant literature. The main *desideratum* for all these systems is self-critical vigilance vis-à-vis their own systems.

THESIS 4: There are efforts to reclaim the Jewishness of Jesus.

The terms "reclaim" and "Jewishness" can be misunderstood. No official statement on Jesus or Christianity is forthcoming from the Grand Rabbi of Jerusalem that we could compare, say, to the Conciliar Declaration on Jewish-Christian relations. But there are books on Jesus by Jewish authors.[8] Such books have had a much greater impact among Christians than among Jews. The reclamation of Jesus' Jewish identity tends to mean a reinterpretation of Jesus in purely Jewish categories. Whatever transcends those categories in the gospels and the New Testament is usually ascribed to the influence of Paul. Each author underscores a different side of this Jewish Jesus: he was close to the Pharisees and was an outstanding and zealous teacher of the Law; he was a Galilean wonder-worker; he was a political agitator like the Zealots and was condemned by the Romans for purely political reasons. The "Third Quest," which is characterized by the unique relevance that it ascribes to Jesus' Jewish origins, also has become associated with this tendency.[9]

THESIS 5: New approaches are also affecting how we see Christ.

I mention just a few main headings:

7. See E. Drewermann, *Tiefenpsychologie und Exegese. I: Die Wahrheit der Formen; II: Die Wahrheit der Werke und der Worte* (Olten: Walter Verlag, 1984/1985). This author has published, among other works, a commentary on the Gospel of Mark in keeping with these categories (1987/1988).

8. The best known are: Shalom Ben-Chorin, David Flusser, Pinchas Lapide.

9. A typical instance would be: J. P. Meier, *A Marginal Jew: Rethinking the Historical Jesus* (3 vols.) (New York: Doubleday, 1991/1994/2001).

Historical Impact [Wirkungsgeschichte]

Some more recent New Testament commentaries, after exegeting a text using current methods, feature a special section recounting the history of the interpretation of the text based on key examples.[10] Similarly, there is a growing interest in the history of exegesis, especially patristic exegesis. Underlying these approaches is the opinion that the unmediated encounter between a two-thousand-year-old text and a contemporary exegete, even one equipped with an abundance of methodological tools, is not necessarily the only and best way to understand this text correctly. The contemporary exegete is not the first one who has endeavored to understand it. The history of the understanding, or of historical impact, of the text should be taken account of by anyone who is attempting to understand it today.

This also sheds a new light on the relationship between the earthly Jesus and the post-Paschal Christ. After all, the post-Paschal Christ is the earthly Jesus — as understood by the original witnesses. The position that makes everything depend on the historical Jesus, reconstructed through historical scholarship alone, explicitly distances itself from this understanding of the first witnesses and, indeed, wishes to set it aside altogether. If, on the other hand, we know how to appreciate the historical impact of the text correctly, then precisely the understanding of the first witnesses becomes highly important for gaining access to the reality of Jesus.

Rhetorical Analysis of the Text

We mention this only as an example of an approach to the biblical texts that is more literary than historical-critical. Conventional exegesis typically dissects and separates. It divides up the texts into smaller and smaller pieces, and assigns them to more and more layers and sources. Rhetorical analysis presupposes that the text, for example, the text of one of the gospels, is an organic whole. Practitioners attempt to clarify the relations be-

---

10. For example, in the series Evangelisch-Katholischer Kommentar zum Neuen Testament (Zürich/Neukirchen-Vluyn).

tween the individual parts, their task and place in the whole and for the structure and message of the whole. It goes without saying that I get a very different view of the figure of Christ depending on whether I attempt to see him in light of a single verse, or part of a verse, or of the whole of a gospel.

Canonical Approach

A focus upon the canonical context of the gospel writings enables one to recognize their overall harmony within their diversity; thus, the image of Christ takes on greater wealth than if one were to consider the testimony of only one sacred writer. Moreover, by including the Old and New Testaments, this methodological approach manifests the profound unity in the witness afforded by both parts of the Christian canon.[11]

Methodological Reflection

Methods are the tools the exegete uses to work on his texts. They are the "spectacles" through which he looks at his objects. One does not make progress in the subject matter simply by busying oneself with one's tools. On the other hand, the results of one's work depend essentially on the type of tools one is using. There is thus a constant need to check the "lenses" to make sure that they are not dusty, or tinted, or cut so as to guarantee a distorted image from the outset. Because methods pre-program exegetical options, we pause to say a few more words on this point.

In the 1970s, methodological reflection was especially lively among exegetes. More than anyone else, Peter Stuhlmacher drew attention to the principles and methods of the historical-critical method in the strict

11. A few representative authors are: B. S. Childs, *Old Testament Theology in a Canonical Context* (Philadelphia: Fortress, 1986); *The New Testament as Canon: An Introduction* (Valley Forge, PA: Trinity Press, 1994); J. A. Sanders, *From Sacred Story to Sacred Text: Canon as Paradigm* (Philadelphia: Fortress, 1987); R. Rendtorff, *The Canonical Hebrew Bible: A Theology of the Old Testament* (Leiden: Deo Publishing, 2005 [original: 1999-2001]).

sense.[12] It works mainly with three criteria in order to sift out the probable from the improbable in what the sources narrate: critique, analogy, and correlation.[13]

Critique is a formal criterion. It stipulates that everything the sources recount and attest to must be put to question and pass through the mill of criticism.

Analogy is the decisive criterion relative to content. It takes the sum of the events we have experienced as the measure of all events in general — what happens around us and in us, the normal, ordinary, or at least well-attested happenings, and states that we know are the fixed reference-point by means of which we separate the possible from the impossible. Whatever in the narrative squares with this criterion can be regarded as possible. Whatever diverges from it has to be seen as impossible and, therefore, cannot have happened in the past.

There is a basic problem with this criterion of analogy. By what right do we elevate the normal, ordinary course of events as we experience them today to the criterion of the possible *tout court?* By what right can we exclude the "extraordinary" as a matter of principle? Troeltsch argues that all events have to be in principle of the same type. He appeals to the "metaphysical assumption that the universe hangs together as a single whole" and to the Deistic conception of God. It hardly comes as a surprise when this criterion leads practitioners to sift out fundamental points of the New Testament's witness concerning Christ, such as his Resurrection, his divine Sonship, and his absolute authority, and to claim that a Christ without these features is the outcome of biblical scholarship. In reality, this outcome is decided in advance by the criterion of analogy itself.

There is little point in debating these results as such. What needs to be scrutinized are the criterion itself and its philosophical basis. By the same token, we are no longer dealing here with an intra-exegetical problem that is best solved using exegetical methods. Philosophers and dogmatic

---

12. P. Stuhlmacher, *Vom Verstehen des Neuen Testaments. Eine Hermeneutik* (GNT 6) (Göttingen: Vandenhoeck & Ruprecht, ²1986 [1st ed., 1979]), pp. 24-26.

13. For a classic presentation of these principles and presuppositions, see E. Troeltsch, "Über historische und dogmatische Methode in der Theologie" (1898), in G. Sauter, ed., *Theologie als Wissenschaft* (ThBüch 43) (München: Kaiser, 1971), pp. 105-27.

theologians have an important contribution to make to the discussion. But it should also be clear to what extent the picture of Christ one takes away from the sources depends on one's method, and how important reflection on one's method is.

A third criterion alongside critique and analogy is *correlation*. Underlying this third criterion is the conviction that every event is consistent with every other, that nothing happens out of the blue, and that nothing ever disappears without leaving any trace. If something recounted in the sources withstands the test of analogy, it has to be submitted to this further trial. It is necessary to verify the preparation for, and after-effects of, the event in the context in which it is supposed to have occurred. Something corresponding to what we said about analogy is also true of the criterion of correlation: analogy tests possibility in itself; correlation tests possibility within context.

Possible Directions for Exegetical Work on Christ

The fundamental *desideratum* is: to know the real Jesus as a whole. We want our view of the real Jesus as a whole to be unobstructed either by our own methods or by the imposition of any overlay on the sources. Achieving this task seems to me to require the following dispositions:

First Guideline: Less Violence with the Sources

The rigorous, rigid application of fixed principles, and of a fixed understanding of history and reality, brings with it the great risk of doing violence to the text.

Comparison with another field will illustrate this point. With regard to humanity's dealings with nature, there is a growing awareness that all one-sided, irreverent, and violent action recoils on us, destroying the environment, and so the foundations, of our own life. Whenever we approach nature with pre-set plans and goals, try to refashion it in our own image, and subjugate it to ourselves, the consequences are not usually immediately apparent. But they are not long in coming. The desolation, devastation, and poisoning of the environment in which we live are not far behind. It thus becomes obvious that careful, respectful treatment of nature is also for our own good.

Analogous to violent encroachments on nature are narrowly fixed interests and principles that render it impossible to perceive the abundant, manifold relations — the cosmos — constituted by the biblical texts. Here, too, the consequences are not always immediately noticeable. But can we not say that pale, weak images of Christ are all that remain when he is drained of his fullness of life — when he is no longer the "chief who leads" (Acts 3:15) us to life, but is dead and leaves us cold?

Here, too, then — to stay with our image — we need an "ecological revolution," a shift towards care, reverence, respect, docility, patience. In our dealings with Scripture, our fundamental attitude should be a refusal to dictate what it may and may not say, what it can and cannot mean, who Christ has to be and who he — according to our *a prioris* — cannot be. The communication should be of such a kind as to let Scripture speak its word openly and freely, to let Christ's person become visible as it really is in its integrity.

Second Guideline: More Trust in the Unique Form of the Sources

A simple comparison of the gospels shows that they are not stenographic reports of the utterances and speeches of Jesus or chronicles that recount his deeds in their chronological and spatial sequence. Obviously, they contain what Jesus actually said and did. But they also contain much that took shape in traditions antedating the evangelists or was formulated by the evangelists themselves on the basis of what they may have come to understand after the original events transpired. Both dimensions — what comes directly from Jesus himself and what comes from witnesses who lived after Jesus — are woven together so tightly as to be separable only with difficulty, if at all.

Our fundamental *desideratum* is to know Jesus as he really is in the integrity of his person. Now, it is widely believed that, in order to do so, we have to read the gospels against the grain. The gospels are used as quarries. Jesus and his deeds are extracted from them in their pure form, or at least that is the intention. The very thing that the gospels do not give us we must laboriously, if only fragmentarily, retrieve from them: "the audio and video recordings," the "stenographic transcripts" of Jesus in action, now "freed" from the perspective of the gospel writers. These, so it seems, are what is indispensable for getting at the real Jesus.

The question arises whether these "audio and video recordings" — even supposing that it is possible to reconstruct with a certain probability sufficiently long segments free from background noise and distortion — are indeed the best way to get at the real Jesus. Do not the gospels, in the unique form we have described just now, correspond much better to the whole character of how Jesus actually acted and what he actually intended?

It is clear that the gospels are not stenographic reports. It is equally clear that Jesus neither wrote any books nor ordered any stenograms. We have no evidence that one of Jesus' chief concerns was to have his words preserved with literal exactitude. But Jesus did gather a circle of disciples, who accompanied him on all his journeys and were under the constant influence of his person. The real Jesus is never isolated and alone. Rather, he always lives in communion with his disciples. He does not want literal exactness. What he wants is for these living men to understand him and to be shaped by him.

Generally speaking, words and deeds are not the only things that come from a person and give us a glimpse into who he is. The same is also true of the impression that he makes on other people — especially when he shares his life with them — and that is formulated, and attested to, by them. The impression and understanding grounded in this real, and not merely verbal, communication sometimes are not, and cannot be, formulated either at the moment of encountering this person or during the period of immediate communion with him, but become clarified only with time — and, despite this time lapse, still find a valid, truthful verbal expression.

Jesus, then, is inseparable from the disciples. The first, fundamental instrument Jesus uses to communicate himself actively is his presence with the disciples and then, in the context of this presence, his words and deeds. Analogously, what remains of Jesus after Easter — besides the presence of

97

his Spirit — are not just collections of authentic words and exactly re-corded deeds. Primarily, it is the living human beings who had the grace of knowing his person and his message in a community of life with him. Jesus did not act with an eye to documentation, but to living testimony. He is re-ceived, and remains alive, not in stenographic transcripts, but in witnesses.

The *reason* for this doubtless lies in the nature of what Jesus has to communicate. Jesus teaches and helps and heals. But what he brings and makes possible in all of that is a new way of living based upon a new rela-tionship to God. Jesus communicates this new way of living in sharing a community of life with his disciples. He calls the disciples to follow him. He makes them traveling companions along a common way, with a com-mon goal, so that they share in his relationship with God. And the disci-ples have to grasp whom they are dealing with in the person of Jesus and what sort of relationship he has to God, not out of some theoretical inter-est, but so that they can adequately grasp this gift, this community of life — for the sake of more life. The disciples' efforts, not only to hand on Je-sus' words, but to speak adequately of Jesus' person, are founded in the na-ture and goal of the communion that Jesus has given them, which is to live in a new relationship to God.

The point would be to consider whether the *unique character of the gos-pels* corresponds to the real Jesus' *characteristic mode of activity* and his goals. Does not the gospels' unique character lead us to the real Jesus?

The gospels are an almost inseparable interweaving of what comes di-rectly from Jesus and what comes from the witnesses who lived on after him. As such, it should be seen both as an account of *what Jesus did in word and deed* [*Wirken Jesu*] and as a record of *the effect Jesus had* [*Wirkung Jesu*] through living encounter and communion — whether with his first, imme-diate disciples or with those who became disciples through them (cf. Matt 28:19f.). Thanks to this connection and this unique character, the gospels correspond to the primordial form of Jesus' active presence, in which the acting Jesus and the disciples who experience the effect of his action are al-ways already bound up together. Because the gospels, whether as an ac-count of what Jesus did or as a record of the effect he had, derive as a whole from Jesus, they also lead to Jesus himself, as he truly was, and they do this as a whole, without any hypothetical separation of what comes from him and what comes from his witnesses.[14] It seems, then, that anyone desirous of knowing the real Jesus, his real intentions, and his real message, should listen as attentively as possible to the gospels, indeed, the whole New Testament, as it has been transmitted to us. The very fact that there are four gospels, each differing in form from the others, is a testimony to the richness of Jesus' person.

Third Guideline: Painstaking Historical Work

This point should be mentioned in order to avoid a misunderstanding. One might ask, in fact, what need remains for the whole exegetical enterprise, if attentive listening to the texts in their present form is sufficient for easy access to the real Jesus. In response, we must not forget that these texts are almost two thousand years old. On the subject of attentive listening, it is just that this demands respecting the texts as historical realities, as realities of their time and environment, which in turn requires us to refrain from imposing our concepts, questions, and expectations upon them. By the same token, there is need for a multifaceted work of exegesis that endeavors to understand the original form of the text (textual criticism), the original language (vocabulary, constructions, special terminologies, expressions, and syntactical patterns current at the time), the intellectual background, the conditions prevailing during its composition (the Jewish and Hellenistic milieu), the authors and their intentions, the addressees and their situation, the history of the interpretation of the texts under consideration, and so forth. This list lays no claim to completeness. It is merely meant to show how an exegesis that aims to listen to the texts is obliged to do historical work.

14. This is a point recently made by James Dunn, who affirms that "the Gospel traditions provide a clear portrayal of the remembered Jesus since they still display with sufficient clarity for present purposes the impact which Jesus made on his first followers": J. D. G. Dunn, *Jesus Remembered* (Christianity in the Making 1) (Grand Rapids/Cambridge: Eerdmans, 2003), p. 6.

Fourth Guideline: The Whole as the Reference-Point

It is very important, precisely for Christology, to avoid any narrow focus on individual verses, or parts of verses, and to keep open instead the question of the overall tendency of the New Testament writing in question, accepting it as the integral whole that it is. For example, if one attempts to understand the title "Son of God" as it appears in just one verse, or part of a verse, it is almost impossible to say whether it remains within the limits of the Old Testament's theology of kingship, and expresses God's special election of the king or Messiah, or whether it transcends those limits in the direction of what we call divine sonship in a metaphysical sense. If we keep our eyes on the character of the gospel as a whole, we will find the answer more easily. Let us show this using the following example.

Christ in John and Mark

No one denies that John's gospel presents us with a so-called "high Christology." The very first verse asserts the pre-existence and divinity of the Logos: "In the beginning was the Word, and the Word was with God, and the Word was God." And the last verse of the prologue distinguishes Jesus' revelation of God clearly from that of the Old Testament. It declares the novelty of the former: "No one has ever seen God. The only Son, who is God and who rests in the bosom of the Father, has made him known" (John 1:18). Until now, no one has known God through direct contact. Because he is the Son of God, who is equal to God and on a par with him, and who knows him in the most intimate communion, Jesus brings us word about God. The Old Testament knows God as the Creator, whom only creatures stand over against. Through Jesus, God makes himself known as a "we" that already exists on the divine level itself, as a communion of Father, Son, and Spirit. God now makes himself known as a God who not only gives men the gifts of creation, but also wishes to adopt them as his children into communion with his Son (cf. John 1:12).

Does Mark's Christology offer anything comparable to this? He makes no explicit declaration about Jesus' pre-existence. In a few passages, he speaks of the Son of God or of God's beloved Son. But the question is precisely how these statements are to be understood. Before we leave this question undecided, or say that Mark goes no further than a simple Messiah Christology, we should take account of the following three observations concerning the character of Mark's gospel as a whole:

All of God's Relations to Men Are Mediated to Them through Jesus

Mark's Gospel speaks of God's kingly rule, of God's commandment, of God's house, and of God's power and glory. All of these terms have to do with definite forms of God's relation to men: his kingly, shepherding care and rule; his binding will; his presence; the definitive revelation of his glory.

The message that God's kingly rule is at hand stands as a kind of motto over Jesus' entire activity (cf. Mark 1:14f.). In that activity, the nearness of God's kingly rule shows itself and comes to pass.

Jesus goes beyond the Old Testament commandments; he requires us to follow him, and makes this an essential condition of life and salvation (cf. Mark 8:34-38; 9:7; 10:17-31). God's will reveals itself in Jesus' person and destiny.

The Risen Lord is the temple not made by hands. He is the definitive place where God is present and accessible to men (cf. Mark 14:58; 15:38).

In Jesus' coming at the end of time, God's power and glory are proclaimed to all men (cf. Mark 8:38; 13:26; 14:62).

All of this raises the question: What sort of relation to God does someone have, who in his person binds together all of God's relations to men, and in whom all of these relations become personally present? Does "Son of God" mean a purely human Messiah?

Mark Is Concentrated on the Christological Question

From the opening citation from Isaiah on, Mark stands in the closest relation to the Old Testament, and he professes its faith in the one Lord and

God (cf. Mark 12:29, 32). Yet the structure and themes of the gospel distinguish it from any type of writing we find in the Old Testament. It is neither a collection of laws, prophetic utterances, or sapiential discourses, nor a narration of the history of king and people. It describes Jesus' activity in the circle of his disciples. And, from the very first verse, which declares *the* content of the Good News to be "Jesus is the Christ the Son of God," it is concentrated, both in question and in answer, on the problem of Jesus' identity: Who is he?

The Old Testament never poses this question about anyone — either Moses, or David, or any of the prophets; even less are any of its writings concentrated on such a person and question. By contrast, the real interest and the real message of Mark's gospel revolve around the identity of Jesus. It is not Jesus' doctrine or praxis, but his person, that is (wholly) in the center. Once again we have to ask: When the evangelist says "Son of God" — does he mean a purely human Messiah?

Mark Preserves the Christological Question

Mark does not simply give the Christological answer to this question. He does not simply report the finished conclusion. He also preserves the whole process of groping, erringly and searchingly, towards Christology.

He highlights *the disciples' lack of understanding* and Jesus' insistent *admonition to understand* (cf. Mark 6:52; 8:17-21). He thereby underscores the difficulty and importance of understanding him properly. What is at issue here is neither obvious nor trivial. In the same way, the radical *rejection* of Jesus' claim by his adversaries is another index of the seemingly intolerable scope of this claim (cf. Mark 14:61-64).

Jesus' *commands not to speak* reveal the problem of incomplete knowledge of Christ and of unenlightened talk about Christ (cf. Mark 8:30; 9:9). Only the experience of the entire trajectory of Jesus' life — including the Cross and the Resurrection — makes it possible to speak correctly about him.

Also significant are the *open-ended pericopes,* which conclude with the disciples and Jesus asking the Christological question: "Who is this, that the wind and sea obey him?" (Mark 4:41); and "David himself calls him 'Lord.' How, then, can he be his son?" (Mark 12:37). The Christological question thus remains open as an enduring task. It is the question that is raised in the disciples by their experience of Jesus' action. And it is the question with which Jesus himself counters all the questions that others have posed to him.

In this way, Mark seems to be insisting that the finished Christological answer is not the end of the story, that Jesus' identity, even when it is correctly named, remains an inexhaustible mystery, which we must constantly inquire into and struggle to understand. From this point of view, too, a purely messianic understanding of the title "Son of God" seems insufficient. "Son of God" does not identify an election, but a unique origin from God.

Mark and John certainly differ in the degree of explicitness with which they present the mystery of Christ. But it seems to me that Mark has an extremely lively sense for this mystery — and that, in this respect, he is hardly inferior to John. Perhaps this example will help to illustrate my earlier point: attention to the whole of a writing can be decisively important for facilitating understanding of what it says about Christ.

*   *   *

Our goal has been to know Jesus, as he really is and as a whole. I believe that we can attain this goal only with, and not against, our sources (which are primarily the four gospels). We have the four gospels. We have the richness of their testimony. Only in an attitude of increasing readiness to hear and perceive do we give the sources the chance to speak their word fully and clearly: to bear witness to the person of Jesus in its richness and its mystery.

Translated by Adrian Walker & Jeff Lawrence

The Reception in the Church of the Dogmatic Constitution "Dei Verbum"

Albert Cardinal Vanhoye

Of the Dogmatic Constitution *Dei Verbum* it has been written that it is "one of the most beautiful texts of the Council's work."[1] The quality of the text, as we know, was the fruit of a long process. It was drawn up over a long period, at times quite troubled, but throughout which there was great perseverance. It had its point of departure in the proposal of a schema at the very first session of the Council, in 1962, with the meaningful title of *"De fontibus revelationis."* The plural *"fontibus"* seemed to be directed towards a plurality of sources of Revelation, or rather, more precisely, a duality, "Scripture" and "Tradition," understood as two sources, each separate from the other. This schema was to bring about some debate afterwards, but it was finally rejected by a large majority (1,368 votes to 822) on 19 November 1962. This rejection was an expression of a decisive option in favor of a unifying perspective. But it would not prove easy to produce a text that would totally satisfy. A special commission, instituted by Pope John XXIII, failed to do so on its first attempt in 1963. It was to be more fortunate in its second attempt, which led to a doctrinally richer redaction. Debated in 1964, during the third session of the Council, this redaction gave rise to numerous remarks, but it did not meet any real opposition. It could then after a careful

---

1. J.-J. Weber, "La Révélation," in *Concile Oecumenique Vatican II* (Paris: Centurion, 1966), p. 34.

revision be brought to a vote, paragraph by paragraph, in 1965, during the fourth and last session of the Council. The numerous "modi" made another revision necessary. The decisive general vote took place on 18 November 1965, less than three weeks before the end of the Council. Of the 2,350 voters, there were only six negative votes.

Scripture and Word of God

The *incipit "Dei Verbum"* draws attention immediately to *the Word of God*. This affords me the opportunity straightaway to mention an unsatisfactory aspect of the reception of the dogmatic Constitution *Dei Verbum*. People often speak of this Constitution as if its subject matter were limited to declarations on Sacred Scripture; the expression *"Dei Verbum"* is thus understood as the *written* Word of God. This, however, is an inexact interpretation, which does not correspond to the intention of the Council Fathers. They meant to situate Scripture in a larger framework, that of the entire economy of salvation. The official title of the Conciliar text is not *"Constitutio dogmatica de Sacra Scriptura"* but rather *"Constitutio dogmatica de Divina Revelatione,"* and the Council specifies that Divine Revelation is transmitted at the same time by Tradition and Scripture, under the authority of the Magisterium (DV 10). The phrase of the Council which states that Magisterium "is not above the Word of God, but serves it" (DV 10) is easily understood as expressing a duty of docility towards Sacred Scripture alone. Again, this is an inexact interpretation, as the preceding phrase specifically mentions Tradition alongside Scripture in using the expression *"verbum Dei scriptum vel traditum"*: "the task of authentically interpreting the word of God, *whether written or handed on*, has been entrusted exclusively to the living teaching office of the Church, whose authority is exercised in the name of Jesus Christ" (DV 10). The word *"traditum"* comes back in the very phrase that expresses a duty of docility towards the Word of God; this docility, it is said, consists in only teaching "what has been handed on" (*"quod traditum est"*). In the context, we realize that that which has been handed down includes Scripture and Tradition at the same time, or, otherwise said, Tradition takes in Scripture.

When the Council defines Scripture (DV 9), it does not say "*Sacra Scriptura est verbum Dei,*" as some translations would lead one to believe, but rather it says "*Sacra Scriptura est* locutio Dei, *quatenus, divino afflante Spiritu, scripto consignatur*" ("Sacred Scripture is *the speaking of God,* inasmuch as it is consigned to writing under the inspiration of the divine Spirit"). It seems that the Council wanted to avoid too tight an identification between "Sacred Scripture" and "Verbum Dei." This latter expression is used immediately afterwards, but in relation to Tradition, which is a confirmation of this perspective: "The Holy Tradition transmits the Word of God (*Verbum Dei*) in its entirety" (DV9). Once again, we are led to believe that Tradition takes in Scripture.

The expression chosen by the Council to define Scripture is surprising, because, taken literally, it affirms that the written text is, in fact, an action of speaking, "*locutio*"; the rest of the phrase accentuates this effect of surprise, as the verb "*consignare*" is placed there in the present tense and not in the past, as one may have expected. The Special Commission had actually placed there the past participle "*consignata,*" which seemed more logical, as the putting into writing of the divine message is a fact in the past; however, the use of "*consignata*" was criticized because, according to Alberto Franzini, "this way of saying it could suggest an identification of the Word of God with its written form."[2] In truth, I do not really understand how this ambiguity could be brought about, or how the present tense "*consignatur*" might remedy it. However, I note this worry about avoiding such confusion. The result is that Sacred Scripture is not defined in its final form, as a text already separated from its author, but in the moment of its being put into writing, as a "living act" — the expression is from Roger Schutz and Max Thurian[3] — a living act that we are in the process of recording. In the end, the conciliar definition leads to a reversal of the relationships between the written text and the oral message. The word "locutio" normally designates an oral message; it is applied by the Council to a written text, the text of the Bible.

One must also note that the Council does not reserve the expression

---

2. A. Franzini, *Tradizione e Scrittura. Il contributo del Concilio Vaticano II* (Brescia: Morcelliana, 1978), p. 193.

3. "Un acte vivant": R. Schutz and M. Thurian, *La parole vivante au Concile* (Taizé: Presses de Taizé, 1966), p. 120; quoted by A. Franzini, *Tradizione e Scrittura,* p. 216.

"verbum Dei" to Tradition; it uses it also for Scripture. I have already quoted the phrase from paragraph 10 which speaks of *"verbum Dei scriptum vel traditum"* designating Scripture as *"verbum Dei scriptum"* and the content of Tradition as *"verbum Dei traditum."* In the last chapter of *Dei Verbum*, it is said that "the Divine Scriptures" "communicate in an unalterable form God's own Word" (*"verbum ipsius Dei,"* DV 21), that they "contain the Word of God and, as they are inspired, they are truly the Word of God" (*"verbum Dei"* twice, DV 24). The French translation published by the Éditions du Centurion avoided the repetition of the words *"verbum Dei"* but it has, in the same way, changed the sense of the affirmation by saying: "The Sacred Scriptures contain the Word of God and, because they are inspired, they are truly *this* word," which brings us back to saying that the Scriptures are *the* Word of God and therefore to affirming a complete identification. The Italian translation in the *L'Osservatore Romano*, reprinted by the *Edizioni Dehoniane*, seems to me to be more faithful to the intentions of the Council, as it omits the article before *"parola di Dio"* (Word of God) and thus avoids a complete identification between the Scriptures and the Word of God. The Scriptures are "word of God"; they are not the entire word of God, but only the written word of God, *"verbum Dei scriptum,"* and so they leave space for the word of God transmitted orally, *"verbum Dei traditum."* Let us say immediately that we are not dealing here with a simple juxtaposition, as the formula I have just used might lead one to believe. Between *"verbum Dei scriptum"* and *"verbum Dei traditum,"* the Council expresses some very close and some very complex relationships.

Scripture and Tradition

With regard to this, I think it useful to highlight another error that can slip into our interpretation of the Council quite easily. Because the Council Fathers rejected, with a good majority, the initial schema, which was entitled *"De Fontibus Revelationis"* and which spoke of sources of Revelation in the plural, one may think that the Council took the option for one single source of Revelation and that that unique source could only be Scripture.

This is a serious misunderstanding. The position of the Council is clearly different. One thing is precise: the Council carefully avoided speaking in the plural of "sources" of Revelation, but we must not forget that it equally carefully avoided presenting Scripture as the unique source of Revelation, an attitude that would have transformed Christianity into a "religion of the Book." That which the Council rejected was the idea of a dichotomy, which would put a duality at the origins of Revelation and which would then keep watertight partitions between Tradition and Scripture. The Council wanted, rather, to insist on the unity of origin and on the multiple connections that keep Scripture and Tradition in a symbiosis. In order to affirm this unity of origin, all Vatican II had to do was to follow the Council of Trent, which puts the word "source" (*"fons"*) in the singular and applies it neither to Scripture nor to Tradition, but to a reality that precedes both and is called "Gospel" (DH 1501; EB 57), not, obviously, used in the sense of one of our four gospels, but rather with the meaning given it by the Apostle Paul where he speaks of "the Gospel, the power of God for the salvation for every believer" (Rom 1:16). Of this Gospel the Council of Trent says, and Vatican II repeats this, that it had been "promised beforehand by the mediation of the Prophets" and that Christ "promulgated it from his own mouth" (DH 1501; DV 7). Vatican II, however, makes two significant additions to the text of Trent. The first is to affirm that in the Lord Jesus "all the Revelation of the Most High God finds its fulfillment." The second is to say that Christ not only promulgated the Gospel, but he "accomplished" it. These two additions make the step from a perspective of simple proclamation of the Truth to a perspective of accomplishing the reality. Thus they give to the Gospel a denser content. Vatican II once again accords with Trent to state that the Gospel is "the source of every salvific truth and every moral rule." If, therefore, it is the source of everything, it is a unique source and one cannot speak of two sources.

Immediately after affirming the existence of this single unique source, the Council of Trent affirms that the content of the Gospel comes to us by a double canal, formed, on one side, "by the written books," and, on the other, "by the non-written traditions" (DH 1501). Vatican II says the same thing, but in other terms and in the inverse order, naming in the first place "the oral preaching" of the Apostles, and in second place the writing down of the message of salvation (DV 7). This inverted order is more conformed to the historical reality, because the oral preaching preceded the writing of the gospels by a few years. It follows, then, that we can say that the Sacred Scripture is the daughter of the Oral Tradition.

Vatican II, as is well known, insists enormously on the union that exists between Scripture and Tradition. It declares that "Sacred Tradition and Sacred Scripture are linked and communicate closely between one another" (DV 9), and it adds: "Both of them, flowing from the same divine wellspring, in a certain way merge into a unity *(in unum . . . coalescunt)* and tend toward the same end." In this phrase, the word is not *"fons"* ("source") but rather the less usual term *"scaturigo"* ("wellspring"), a more dynamic term, which expresses a gushing forth. In another passage, however, the Council also uses a static metaphor, that of the "deposit" (1 Tim 6:20; 2 Tim 1:14), when it affirms that "Sacred Tradition and Sacred Scripture form one sacred deposit of the Word of God, committed to the Church" (DV 10). The metaphors are very different but the basic affirmation remains the same: it concerns the union of Scripture and Tradition. In this we see that the rejection of the theory of two sources in no way means a rejection of Tradition in favor of Scripture alone: rather this signifies a refusal of any separation between Tradition and Scripture.

The Council gives a definition of Sacred Scripture. It says that it is "The speaking of God [*locutio Dei*], inasmuch as it is consigned to writing under the inspiration of the divine Spirit" (DV 9). In the same passage, it does not define what Tradition is but what it *does*. It transmits: ". . . while Sacred Tradition takes the Word of God entrusted by Christ the Lord and the Holy Spirit to the Apostles, and hands it on to their successors in its full purity" (DV 9). This definition takes the word *traditio* in its first meaning, which expresses the action of transmitting, a dynamic aspect. On the other hand, the phrase expresses also the content that Tradition transmits: "the Word of God entrusted to the Apostles."

Another passage of *Dei Verbum* shows that this "Word of God" should not be conceived as an inert mass, but as energy for life. It actually says that "with the assistance of the Holy Spirit," Tradition "progresses" (*"proficit,"* DV 8), yet another dynamic aspect. The Council so explains that the perception of the content of Tradition grows constantly, due to contemplation and study, due to personal experience of the spiritual life, and to the preaching of the bishops (DV 8).

The connection between Tradition and Scripture appears quite strong. One can say, it seems to me, that Scripture is part of the content of Tradition, as it is transmitted in the Church from generation to generation, and the fixing of the Canon of the Sacred Books in particular was part of the growth of Tradition. The Council recalls this important fact: "Through the same tradition the Church's full Canon of the Sacred Books is known"; and it adds: ". . . and [through it] the Sacred Writings themselves are more profoundly understood and unceasingly made active in her" (DV 8). That which is said, in the last chapter of *Dei Verbum*, concerning the efforts of "the Church, taught by the Holy Spirit" in order to "move ahead toward a deeper understanding of the Sacred Scriptures" (DV 23) is therefore to be attributed to the dynamism of the Tradition.

Although they have their origin in Tradition, the Scriptures are superior to it in that they are directly inspired by God and are connected immediately, in the New Testament, to the foundational period of the history of salvation. This direct inspiration and this immediate link have as a consequence that the Scriptures — I am quoting the Council — are to be found "once and for all consigned to writing" and "they communicate in an unalterable form the Word of God and they sound forth in the words of the prophets and the apostles the very voice of the Holy Spirit" (DV 21). Nothing of that nature can be said of Tradition. One must add, however, that this superiority of the Scriptures is accompanied by a certain inferiority, which means that the Scriptures need Tradition. Having been fixed in an unalterable form, the Scriptures offer believers an anchor; but this very immutability carries in itself a certain inconvenience. They risk remaining dead letters, as the *Catechism of the Catholic Church* recognizes (n. 108), or even becoming a letter that kills, as the phrase of the Apostle Paul, "the letter kills, it is the Spirit that gives life" (2 Cor 3:6), applies to the Scriptures. So that they might become living and active in the Church, so that they might effectively "sound forth the voice of the Holy Spirit," they have to be carried on the living current of Tradition, a current that has its source in the same Holy Spirit. As A. Franzini has written, "deprived of the ecclesial Tradition, Scripture would be a dead body. The only function to which it could aspire would be of documentary nature,"[4] like texts of ancient historians. After the end of the foundational period, Tradition was to produce no more texts inspired by the Holy Spirit, but it is favored with the assistance of the Holy Spirit to "actualize" the Scriptures, in a double sense: an actualization of knowledge and of efficaciousness, to make the Scriptures understood in the contemporary world and then to make them operative in this present world.

Catholic exegesis cannot ignore this role of Tradition. In its document from 1993 on *The Interpretation of the Bible in the Church*, the Biblical Commission explicitly recognized it. It declares there that that which characterizes Catholic exegesis is "that it consciously situates itself in the living tradition of the Church, the primary care of which is faithfulness to the revelation attested in the Bible" (chapter III, introduction: EB 1424). Far from being anti-scientific, this position corresponds to the needs of modern hermeneutics, particularly with regard to its "pre-understandings." In adopting as its pre-understanding the living tradition of the Church, Catholic exegesis is placing itself in a most favorable position for the authentic interpretation of texts, as these are the fruit of previous steps in the same tradition. This "corresponds to the living affinity between the interpreter and the text which he explains, an affinity which constitutes one of the conditions for the possibility of the exegetical enterprise" (ibid.).

Tradition is not a collection of texts "consigned to writing once and for all," as Scripture is. It is a living current, which adapts itself to circumstances. In this way, along with its many advantages, it runs some risks of weakness. Having resolutely taken a positive perspective, the Council did not draw attention to these risks, and consequently was open to some criticisms.[5]

When it speaks of Tradition, it specifies at times that this is the Tradition "which comes from the Apostles" (DV 8), but immediately it notes that this tradition "progresses in the Church," which means that it assimilates new elements. As a living organism, it cannot remain in existence without renewing itself continually. The problem, therefore, is to remain faithful to its origin through all the changes. The Council calmly affirms

4. A. Franzini, *Tradizione e Scrittura*, p. 211.
5. Cf. A. Franzini, *Tradizione e Scrittura*, pp. 240-57.

that faithfulness has been maintained: from generation to generation "the Church, in her teaching, life and worship, perpetuates . . . all that she herself is, all that she believes" (DV 8). In this very positive affirmation, the Council does not preoccupy itself with mentioning the duty of discernment that is imposed upon the Church in the course of her continual progression. This duty is essential. It is not enough that a belief or a practice becomes "traditional" in the Church so that it is deigned to be an authentic expression of the Apostolic Tradition. Certain traditions have a value limited only to their time and place and can become obstacles to the development of Tradition. Others may never have a real value. Theological reflection and pastoral discernment have a role here in completing the teaching of the Council, which could not deal with all the problems. The intention of the Council Fathers was to note strongly the close union of Tradition and Scripture, their unity of origin, their reciprocal dependence, and their necessary complementarity in order to assure the Church of a stable and life-giving relationship with the Word of God.

Revelation and Communion

Having already considered two themes whose reception was troubled, let us now turn to one that did not pose the same difficulty, Revelation, or more precisely, the way in which *Dei Verbum* presents Revelation. Dom Ghislain Lafont has published a very enlightening study on this subject, from which I will draw significantly here.[6]

From its Preamble, the Constitution *Dei Verbum* announces that, in order to "propose the true doctrine on Divine Revelation," it will follow in the footsteps of the Councils of Trent and Vatican I (*"Conciliorum Tridentini et Vaticani I inhaerens vestigiis"*). Dom Lafont examines therefore where Vatican II situates itself in relation to Trent and Vatican I, and he shows how there was fidelity and innovation at the same time. Vatican II takes up many of the elements offered by the preceding Councils, but it places them

---

6. Gh. Lafont, "La Constitution 'Dei Verbum' et ses précédents conciliaires," in *NRT* 110 (1988): 58-73.

in a new perspective, which, having been prepared in the theological studies previous to Vatican II, were subsequently favorably received.

The decree *Sacrosancta* of the Council of Trent, which deals with "the reception of the sacred books and the traditions of the Apostles" (DH 1501-1505) and the dogmatic constitution *Dei Filius* of the First Vatican Council, which deals with the Catholic Faith (DH 3000-3045), both carry a certain polemical aspect. The decree of the Council of Trent was opposed to Protestants, who had rejected as "apocrypha" certain books of the Catholic Bible and who would not hear of Tradition, but proclaimed "*sola Scriptura*" as their principle. As for the Constitution of the First Vatican Council, it is preoccupied with the struggle against rationalism.

The Constitution *Dei Verbum*, on the other hand, does not express any polemic or apologetic aspect. It does not seek to demonstrate the legitimacy or the credibility of Christian Revelation. It is presented as a positive doctrinal exposition and a witness to faith. With regard to this, its opening is very meaningful. It declares: "Hearing the word of God with religious reverence and proclaiming it with faith, the Sacred Synod takes its direction from these words of St. John: 'We announce to you the eternal life which dwelt with the Father and was made visible to us. What we have seen and heard we announce to you, so that you may have fellowship with us and our common fellowship be with the Father and His Son Jesus Christ' (1 John 1:2-3)" (DV 1). Revelation is then presented immediately in a perspective that is not simply intellectual, as were those of Trent and Vatican I, but one of interpersonal existential relationships, a perspective of communion between the human person and the divine persons. This perspective is retaken immediately at the beginning of the first chapter which defines Revelation and says that, by means of same, "the invisible God . . . out of the abundance of His love speaks to men as friends . . . and lives among them . . . , so that He may invite and take them into fellowship with Himself" (DV 2). Revelation has its origin in this overflow of love, "*ex abundantia caritatis suae*," and it has a life in communion of love as a goal. We note that this perspective corresponds perfectly with that of the Bible, where God shows himself with a view to establishing a covenant, and where the expression "to know God" does not mean a simple mental recognition, but rather a coming into relationship with God.

Later, speaking of Sacred Scripture, Vatican II has a wonderful phrase, which overflows with the same meaning as it states: "For in the sacred books, the Father who is in heaven meets His children with great love and speaks with them" (DV 21: "*filiis suis peramanter occurrit*"). After this, the conclusion of *Dei Verbum* can confidently wish that "the treasure of Revelation . . . may more and more fill the hearts of men" (DV 26). A Revelation that has love as its origin and final aim will fill the hearts of those who welcome it.

This welcome will be, obviously, a process in freedom. Love cannot exist without freedom. A comparison between paragraph 5 of *Dei Verbum* and the text it quotes from the First Vatican Council is very revealing in this regard. Vatican I is preoccupied with the idea that faith is reasonable and that it is a moral obligation. The phrase therefore begins with a causal clause: "As humanity depends totally upon God, as Creator and Lord, and as created reason is subject to uncreated truth"; there comes then the affirmation of the obligation: "we are bound to give to the God who reveals a total homage of intelligence and will" (DH 3008). In *Dei Verbum*, the causal clause disappears: it is replaced by brief but decisive recourse to Scripture. This is the "obedience of faith," a Pauline formula taken from Romans 1:5 and 16:26: "The obedience of faith . . . is to be given to God who reveals" (DV 5). The expression of Vatican I, "a total homage of intelligence and will" is preserved in *Dei Verbum*, but it is preceded and followed by two allusions to the freedom of the act of faith and to this aspect of the gift of the entire person. Instead of saying, as Vatican I did, "we are obliged to give a total homage etc.," *Dei Verbum* explains that, by the obedience of faith, "man commits his whole self freely to God, offering the full submission of intellect and will to God who reveals." This phrase greatly broadens our way of conceiving faith, which is no longer presented as an adhesion to certain truths, but an adhesion that involves the entire person (DV 5).

Human freedom finds its scope in history. With regard to this, Dom Lafont observes that, in the presentation of Revelation by *Dei Verbum*, "the taking into account of *history* is essential; this appears as much as a *dimension* of Revelation as of its transmission . . . but also formally as an *element* of Revelation, which is enacted by means of the reciprocity of salvific *deeds* and their revealed *meaning."*[7] *Dei Verbum* speaks specifically of "the history of salvation" (DV 2). Using the text from the Council of Trent which says that the traditions have come "from the mouth of Christ himself" (*"ab ipsius Christi ore"*; DH 1501, EB 57), *Dei Verbum* adds that they have also come "from living with Him, and from what He did," and that the apostles transmitted them "by examples and by institutions" no less than by their preaching (DV 7). Revelation thus passes from the domain of language to that of facts, and so acquires a stronger existential density.

A comparison between the texts on Revelation in Vatican I and Vatican II sheds light on another important difference, which looks at our communion with the mystery of the Trinity. Vatican I states globally that "it was pleasing to God to reveal himself as well as the eternal decrees of his will" (DH 3004); *Dei Verbum* does not content itself with this expression, but modifies it and makes it more specific. Instead of speaking of the "eternal decrees," *Dei Verbum* speaks of *"sacramentum,"* i.e., "mystery," and specifies that this mystery of the divine will consists in the fact that "humanity, through Christ made flesh and in the Holy Spirit, have access to the Father and are brought into participation in the divine nature" (DV 2). This Trinitarian language, nurtured on Sacred Scripture, shows all the existential and interpersonal depth of Revelation, which is not simply a communication of truth, but introduces the most intense communion of love there is. This was, naturally, very favorably received.

Inspiration and Believing Community

When the Constitution *Dei Verbum* speaks of the inspiration of the Sacred Books (DV 11), it does not take up again the theme of communion, but contents itself with a sober calling to mind of the teachings of previous councils. It declares that "Those divinely revealed realities which are contained and presented in Sacred Scripture have been committed to writing under the inspiration of the Holy Spirit" (DV 11). It is to be noted that Vatican II avoided saying *"Spiritu Sancto dictante,"* the formula used by the Council of Trent

---

7. Gh. Lafont, "La Constitution Dei Verbum," p. 61.

and Vatican I, but with regard to Tradition (DH 1501; 3006) and not in reference to Scripture. For Scripture *Dei Verbum* says *"Spiritu Sancto afflante"* in the first sentence of paragraph 11, and then, a little later *"Spiritu Sancto inspirante."* For the role of the Holy Spirit in Tradition, *Dei Verbum* 7 replaces the *"dictante"* of Trent and Vatican I by the word *"suggerente."* In this way the idea of a verbal inspiration is avoided. This idea of a verbal inspiration would have suggested that the choice of words did not at all depend upon the human authors, but solely upon the Holy Spirit. Without entering into any theoretical explanation of the process of inspiration (there is no mention, for example, of the principal cause and the instrumental cause), *Dei Verbum* affirms that the Sacred texts "have God as author" and, at the same time, that the biblical writers are "true authors" (*"veri auctores"*) of their writings, as they made use of "their faculties and their strengths" (DV 11). God, however, mysteriously "acted in them and through them," so that they might transmit in writing "all that he wanted and only that" (DV 11).

This declaration, which limits itself to the essential, leaves the field open to theological research.[8] These studies take into consideration the results of exegetical studies, in particular the importance given to the dynamism of the believing community. No writing is ever a purely individual creation; its production is always linked to its surroundings and to a given situation. The biblical writings do not escape from this conditioning. The *Formgeschichte* method has taught us to seek out their *Sitz im Leben*. In order to better understand the nature of biblical inspiration, one should be attentive to the environment of the production of the biblical writings. Already Karl Rahner has explained inspiration as an aspect of the intervention of God in human history, and more precisely in the history of a community of believers. He writes: "At the same time as God, with an absolute will, formally pre-defining the history of salvation and eschatology, wills and produces the primitive Church and its constitutive elements, he wills and produces Scripture in such a way as he becomes its inspirer and its creator (*Urheber*), its author."[9] This affirmation has the merit of not consider-

---

8. In what follows, I take inspiration from H. Gabel, "Inspiration und Wahrheit der Schrift (DV 11). Neue Ansätze und Probleme im Kontext der gegenwärtigen wissenschaftlichen Diskussion," *ThG* 45 (2002): 121-36.

9. K. Rahner, *Über die Schriftinspiration* (QD 1) (Freiburg: Herder, 1958), p. 58.

ing inspiration as an isolated phenomenon, but rather to present it as a particular aspect of the divine work, more spread out and rooted in history. It has the defect of not saying anything of the Old Testament, or of the salvation of the world. This is a reason why another author, Meinrad Limbeck, has proposed a modification, saying: "At the same time as God wills, with an absolute will, the salvation of all humans through the history of Israel and of the primitive Church, a history he sets in motion by distinguishing it from the ordinary course of events, he wills and produces also the Scripture of the Old and New Testaments, in such a way as he becomes their inspirer and creator, their author."[10]

Another omission in Rahner's phrase concerns the biblical authors. They are not mentioned at all. This omission favors the position of those who attribute the production of the texts to the community rather than to the persons. However, one detail of Rahner's phrase opposes this interpretation: Rahner does not present the primitive church as an undifferentiated collectivity, but he indicates that it has "constitutive elements," among which one must certainly count the Twelve and those who, along with them, were, as the Third Gospel says, "eye-witnesses and servants of the Word" (Luke 1:2). Scriptural inspiration is to be found in continuity with these types of functions, which are accompanied by charisms. It is itself a charism given by God to certain members of the believing community for the service of the Word and for the benefit of the community and of the mission. This charism sets its roots, so to speak, in the faith life of the community and should not be separated from that, but it is not, strictly speaking, a community charism. Exegetical studies lead one to believe, however, that in the production of a given text, the charism can be stretched out over several persons, if they have all contributed to this production. It would be strange to limit inspiration to the final redactor, especially if his role were not so important, and to refuse it to the previous authors, whose contributions were much more substantial. One can speak of a "current" of inspiration, in a way, the action of which is stretched out over different stages in the formation of a text. Certain authors suggest

10. M. Limbeck, "Die Heilige Schrift," in W. Kern, ed., *Handbuch der Fundamentaltheologie*, vol. 4 (Freiburg: Herder, 1988), p. 86.

that one might even admit that this current continued to be active in the work of the translators of the Septuagint, who, in more than one case, added to the text new potentialities.

Certain authors suggest extending the charism of inspiration to readers of the Bible. They move out from noticing that many of the biblical texts owe their production to the *"relecture"* (rereading) of earlier texts. Daniel, for example, composed his text (Dan 9) from a *"relecture"* of an oracle of Jeremiah (Jer 25:11-12). The writings of the New Testament reflect a *"relecture"* of the Old Testament made in the light of the events of the life, death, and resurrection of Jesus. One can conclude from this that inspiration does not only concern the action of writing, but also the action of reading. From this one can draw the consequence that it is suitable to speak also of the inspiration of the readers, who, under the guidance of the Holy Spirit, not only discover the profound meaning of ancient texts, but contribute to them an addition to their meaning. Their action of reading includes an action of creativity. In this sense, Ulrich Körtner has spoken of "the inspired reader"; such is the title of one of his books.[11] Without denying the aspect of creativity that is to be seen in certain ways of reading the Bible, it is good not to confuse them with scriptural inspiration in the strict sense. The inspired reader does not produce new biblical texts that should be entered into the scriptural Canon. This reader's inspiration is involved with the "actualization" of the Bible and the production of texts that express this actualization, but not in the creation of supplements to the Bible. *Dei Verbum* has specified that the People of God need not await any further public revelation (DV 4); this declaration excludes in particular the hypothesis of additions to be made to the Sacred Scriptures, which is public revelation *par excellence*. That said, one must recognize that in becoming conscious of the close relations that bind scriptural inspiration to the community of believers, recent studies have opened up enlightening and worthwhile perspectives.

---

11. U. H. J. Körtner, *Der Inspirierte Leser. Zentrale Aspekte biblischer Hermeneutik* (Göttingen: Vandenhoeck & Ruprecht, 1994).

Biblical Studies and Theology

In its last chapter *Dei Verbum* deals with "Sacred Scripture in the life of the Church" and it expresses, in excellent terms, the importance of the Bible for the spiritual life of believers, "jointly with Tradition." The written Word of God constitutes "the support and energy of the Church, the strength of faith for her sons, the food of the soul, the pure and everlasting source of spiritual life" (DV 21); in this regard, it mentions translations and it shows itself favorable to ecumenical translations (DV 22). This suggestion of the Council has not rested a dead letter. In many countries, Catholics have collaborated with Protestants and with Orthodox Christians to carefully prepare common translations and to publish them, something that has proved to constitute important progress on the road to unity.

The Council encourages, on another level, the reading of the Bible and the meditation thereupon. It addresses this encouragement firstly "to all the clergy," "especially the priests," but also to all Christians (DV 25). These words of the Council have had many repercussions. I shall not elaborate on this subject; I content myself here to call to mind the strong impetus that Cardinal Martini has given, within his diocese and elsewhere, to the *"Lectio divina,"* that is, the attentive reading of a biblical text *(lectio),* followed by a time of reflection on the import of this text upon Christian life *(meditatio),* then a time of prayer, addressed to God the Father or to Christ *(oratio),* and finally a time of union to God in the *contemplatio.* Cardinal Martini has said: "without *lectio divina,* there is no deepened Christian life."[12] The Constitution *Dei Verbum* does not employ the expression *lectio Divina,* but it uses equivalent formulae: *"assidua lectio sacra," "frequens divinarum Scripturarum lectio," "pia lectio,"* and it invites the faithful to "remember that prayer must accompany the reading of the Sacred Scripture so that there might be a dialogue between God and humanity" (DV 25). Such is very much the program of the *Lectio divina.*

It seems useful to elaborate one last point, i.e., the relationship between biblical studies and theology. On this point, Dei Verbum took up, with some modification, a desire expressed by Leo XIII in his encyclical

---

12. C. M. Martini, *Perché Gesù parlava in parabole?* (Bologna: Dehoniane, 1985), p. 108.

Providentissimus Deus (1893) and repeated by Benedict XV in *Spiritus Paraclitus* (1920). Leo XIII declared it "highly desirable, and even necessary, that the use of Divine Scripture should have an influence on all the discipline of theology, and should almost be the soul thereof."[13] Leo XIII spoke of the "use" of Scripture (in Latin *"usus"*). *Dei Verbum* speaks of the "study" (*"studium"*) and wishes that "the study of the *Sacra Pagina* should be as the soul of *Sacra Theologia*" (DV 24). This new formulation makes the necessary relationship between theology and exegesis more explicit. In effect, if for "using" Scripture it was enough to quote the text, to "study" Scripture means making exegetical studies, either personally or in putting oneself in the schools of the professional exegetes. In the end, the phrase of the Council demands that exegesis should be *as* the soul of theology. The comparative conjunction "as" thankfully tones down this affirmation. In effect, if exegesis has a certain role of animation in relation to theology, it cannot truly be its soul. Theology is *"fides quarens intellectum"*; its soul therefore is the breath of faith, which comes from the Holy Spirit.

This wish of *Dei Verbum* still retains a great importance. Its influence provoked a renewal in theological research and in the teaching of theology. In order to demonstrate this, some long developments would be necessary. It seems more opportune to me to draw attention to the requirement that results from this wish for exegesis itself. As the document of the Biblical Commission says (III, D2: EB 1492), if it is true that "in order to interpret Scripture with scientific exactness and precision, theologians need the work of exegetes," it is also true that "for their part, exegetes should direct their studies in such a way that 'the study of Sacred Scripture' can effectively be 'as the soul of theology' (DV 24)." This supposes that exegesis itself should be, like the other theological disciplines, *"fides quaerens intellectum,"* an intellectual study practiced with a pre-understanding of faith. *Dei Verbum* gives exegetes very clear indications in this direction in its paragraph 12, which deals with the interpretation of Scripture. It cannot be said that its teaching was received properly by all Catholic exegetes. What is said there on the study of literary genres, which *Dei Verbum* approves, as the encyclical *Divino Afflante Spiritu* had done, was greeted warmly. Less earnestness was seen in welcoming the other part of the same paragraph, which invites exegetes to place themselves in a spiritual perspective, "in order to discover correctly the meaning of the Sacred Texts."

A strong tendency, provoked by their relations with unbelieving exegetes and scholars, pushes Catholic exegetes to adopt a strictly scientific perspective, neutral with regard to faith. Instead of being a theological discipline, exegesis is reduced to being a historico-philological study of ancient texts. A fairly recent article from a Catholic exegete clearly expresses this position[14] and presents it as the normal position of every Catholic exegete.

The author asks the exegete "to try to wipe away his subjectivity, to put on hold his faith and its misgivings" (p. 152). "Because it is an autonomous exercise of human reason, exegesis . . . cannot make space for faith in its operations and in its criteria" (p. 157). The exegete must look only for the human meaning of the text, with the sole criteria of human reason. "Having come to an understanding of the human and contingent meaning of the text, the exegete passes it on to the theologian, the integral interpreter, to whom it belongs to show how this human meaning is really Word of God" (p. 159). Such a division of work does not at all correspond to the doctrine of the Council, and it is even challenged by non-Catholic exegetes. Brevard Childs, for example, has noted that, if exegesis is not practiced "within an explicit faith setting," it cannot be useful for theology, because "it is impossible to build a bridge which would go from a neutral descriptive content to a theological reality."[15]

In order to correctly interpret the Bible, which relates religious experiences and makes a call upon the religious capacities of human persons, the best prescribed basis for departure is the faith experience that is situated in the religious tradition from which the texts have come. Taking inspiration from an affirmation of Saint Jerome,[16] *Dei Verbum* declares with regard to this that "Sacred Scripture should be read and interpreted in the same

---

13. "*Illud autem maxime optabile est et necessarium, ut eiusdem Divinae Scripturae usus in universam theologiae influat disciplinam eiusque prope sit animam*" (EB 114 and 483).

14. J.-M. Sevrin, "L'exégèse critique comme discipline théologique," in *RThL* 21 (1990): 146-62.

15. B. S. Childs, "Interpretation in Faith," in *Int* 18 (1964): 432-49, p. 438; quoted in an unedited contribution of P. D. Barthelemy, O.P., for the work of the Biblical Commission.

16. *In Gal.* 5.19-21 (PL 26, 445).

Spirit in which it has been written" (*"eodem Spiritu quo scripta est"*: DV 12). This is, of course, the Holy Spirit: the sentence of Saint Jerome says it explicitly. In a collective volume on Vatican II, Fr. de la Potterie recalls that this declaration was added late to the text of *Dei Verbum*.[17] Actually, it does not fit perfectly in the sentence where it has been added. While it would make one expect indications concerning the personal attitude of the exegete, it is followed by objective criteria: the attention to be given "to the content and the unity of all the Scriptures, keeping account of the living tradition of the entire Church and the analogy of faith." These criteria are assuredly in relation to the doctrine of inspiration, but they remain in some way outside. Many Council Fathers proposed a more interior explanation, which should be at the basis of objective studies: the reading and the interpretation of the Bible should be done in an attitude of faith. As the Apostle Paul says, it is "when we turn towards the Lord" in faith, that the "veil is lifted and the true meaning of Scripture appears" (cf. 2 Cor 3:16). Fr. de la Potterie has shown well how this conviction is present in Origen, in Jerome, Hilary, Ambrose, and Gregory the Great. The Holy Spirit has given a dimension of interiority to the texts that he inspired; one must let the reader who reads in the light of faith discover this dimension. For one who closes himself in the limits of reason, Scripture remains impossible to assimilate. For one who is docile to the Holy Spirit, the inspired word becomes inspiring, and he discovers little by little its multiple potentialities.

In his discourse from 1993 for the one-hundredth anniversary of *Providentissimus Deus*, Pope John Paul II really underlined this condition for an authentic exegesis. He declared that "in order to arrive at a totally valid interpretation of the words inspired by the Holy Spirit, one must be oneself guided by the Holy Spirit and for that, one must pray, one must pray very much, to ask in prayer for the interior light of the Spirit, to ask for love, which alone makes one capable of understanding the language of God who 'is love' (1 John 4:8, 16). During this same work of interpretation,

---

17. I. de la Potterie, "Interpretation of Holy Scripture in the Spirit in Which It Was Written (*Dei Verbum* 12c)," in R. Latourelle, ed., *Vatican II: Assessment and Perspectives*, vol. 1 (New York: Paulist Press, 1988), pp. 220-66, p. 240 and n. 67.

one must keep oneself as much as possible in the presence of God."[18] These words of the Pope take exactly the counter-position of the exegete whom I quoted above. That is to say that they invite many exegetes to a conversion. We must note that John Paul II in no way encourages exegetes to replace scientific research with pious sentimentalism. Far from weakening the rigors of research and study, the spiritual boost obtained from prayer should favor this study, by stopping the exegete from being content with superficial viewpoints. Brought to a purity of faith, exegesis is guarded from pre-conceived opinions, which might seem linked to faith, but which, in reality, come from human influences and not from docility to the Word of God.

In concluding his study, which we have already quoted, Fr. de la Potterie asks if we can speak of a "reception" of the principle of Vatican II in the modern activity of Catholic exegetes. His response is that "to a great extent, we must answer in the negative."[19] "A purely historical, and therefore secularized, manner of reading the Scriptures predominates today," he writes (p. 256). In effect, we have seen that a certain number of Catholic exegetes deem it necessary, for reasons of method, to exclude faith from exegetical research.[20] However, a certain evolution is being marked out, which is in a direction that favors the reception of the Council. In the volume on Vatican II, Fr. Maurice Gilbert describes it in optimistic terms.[21]

He notes first how much the historical-critical method has evolved. It has lost its original connections with liberal Protestantism. Catholics who use this method do not at all adopt the agnostic or hypercritical positions. Also, the method has opened up to complementary perspectives. The study of literary forms (*Formgeschichte*), which chewed up the text into little units, has been succeeded by the study of the redaction of the text,

18. Discourse of Pope John Paul II on 23 April 1993: *L'Osservatore Romano*, 24.4.1993, p. 7 (EB 1249).

19. I. de la Potterie, "Interpretation of Holy Scripture," p. 255.

20. In truth, towards the end of his article, the author quoted above admits, on the subject of faith, that "to share it with the biblical authors could help us to understand them better"; J.-M. Sevrin, "L'exégèse critique," p. 158.

21. M. Gilbert, "New Horizons and Present Needs: Exegesis Since Vatican II," in *Vatican II: Assessment and Perspectives*, vol. 1, pp. 321-43.

which is more attentive to the general direction of the text. After this came the *Wirkungsgeschichte*, which, in order to better understand the bearing of the text, studies the history of its interpretation and the effects that it has produced over the ages. Therein is a very great broadening of the method, as originally the objective of the method was to establish the meaning of the texts *at the time of their production.* The *Wirkungsgeschichte* brings one to recognize that the text has potentialities that do not appear precisely at the moment of its production, but are to be seen a long time after.

That said, the historical-critical method has lost its monopoly. Other methods and other approaches are now used in order to highlight the value of different aspects of the text (study of the literary structure, rhetorical analysis, and narrative exegesis). Among these innovations some correspond very closely to what the Council asked when it asked exegetes to be attentive "to the content and to the unity of all Scripture, keeping in mind the living Tradition of the entire Church" (DV 12). Several approaches, in effect, are based on Tradition; and the canonical approach "interprets every biblical text in the light of the Canon of Scripture, that is, of the Bible in so far as it is received as the norm of faith for believers."[22]

Fr. Maurice Gilbert records these diverse signs of progress, which bring him to a positive judgment on the present direction of Catholic exegesis. He declares that "the theological significance of the texts, which are the 'rule of faith,' is being increasingly emphasized" (p. 336), and that "there are many exegetes today who are able to transmit the *lectio divina* as recommended by the Second Vatican Council" (p. 338), that "the ability of those in charge of biblical pastoral work has greatly increased," thanks to "a considerable effort" accomplished by exegetes to "provide all the people of God with suitable work tools" (pp. 338-39). Therefore, there has been progress in the direction of "a more theological exegesis" that is "more spiritual," "more pastoral," and also "more ecumenical" (pp. 336-39), to which is also added a "return to ancient exegesis" (p. 335). This vista seems very comforting.

---

22. Biblical Commission, *The Interpretation of the Bible in the Church,* I. C.1 (EB 1326).

Conclusion

We can conclude on this positive note. The dogmatic Constitution on divine Revelation has produced abundant and wholesome fruits. Its reception in the Church has not been perfect, but the insufficiencies I was able to note do not at all compromise the notable overall success. For the future, there is the hope of a greater faithfulness to the teaching of the Council, with its refusal of dichotomies and its care for unity. The Word of God, according to the Council, is not Scripture separated from Tradition, but rather Scripture carried on the life-giving current of Tradition. Revelation is not simply the communication of a collection of truths; it is above all a putting into relations with persons; it introduces people into a life of communion with God — Father, Son, and Spirit. In order to be "as the soul of theology," exegetical study must be attentive to the spiritual depth of the biblical texts, which presupposes, on the part of the exegete, docility to the Holy Spirit. These directions, demanding but enriching, have already shown their fruitfulness. We may add that the Council could not claim to say everything. It left more than one area to the initiative of the researchers. It did not, for example, explore the multiple dimensions of scriptural inspiration. The present situation is, because of this, all the more stimulating and full of promise.

Translated by Sean Maher

Exegesis and the Magisterium of the Church

Joseph Cardinal Ratzinger

I have chosen the topic of my presentation, not only because it belongs objectively among the questions that naturally arise when we look back on these hundred years of the Pontifical Biblical Commission's existence, but also because it is, so to say, one of the problems of my own autobiography. For over half a century, my own theological journey has partly been defined by the field of tensions we delineate when we propose to discuss the issue of exegesis and the Magisterium.

The July 29, 1912, Consistorial Decree *De quibusdam commentariis non admittendis*[1] contains two names that tangentially affected my own life. First of all, the decree condemns Freising professor Karl Holzhey's *Introduction to the Old Testament*. Holzhey had already died before I began to study theology in Freising in 1946, but all sorts of stories continued to circulate about him in the seminary. He must have been a rather arrogant and somewhat gloomy man.

A second individual named in the decree has a closer relation to me: Fritz Tillmann, who is cited as the author of a commentary on the New Testament characterized as unreliable. Tillmann's friend Friedrich Wilhelm Maier, at the time an unsalaried lecturer [*Privatdozent*] at the University of Strasbourg, had agreed to undertake the Synoptics for Tillmann's

---

1. EB 400a.

commentary. The decree of the Consistorial Congregation required that these commentaries *expungenda omnino esse ab institutione clericorum* [were to be altogether expunged from the education of the clergy]. The commentary, of which I discovered a mislaid and forgotten copy in the minor seminary of my hometown of Traunstein, had to be interrupted and withdrawn from the market because Maier had defended the so-called two-source theory (which today is almost universally accepted) as an account of the Synoptic problem.

This also put a temporary end to the academic careers of both Tillmann and Maier. Both were allowed to switch to another theological discipline, however. Tillmann took advantage of this opportunity and became the leading German moral theologian, who co-authored with T. Steinbüchel and T. Müncker a pioneering handbook of moral theology that reconceived, and restructured, this important discipline in terms of the fundamental idea of the following of Christ. Maier declined to take advantage of the chance to change disciplines, since he was devoted heart and soul to New Testament research. He thus became a military chaplain, in which capacity he participated in the First World War. Afterwards, he worked as a prison chaplain. Finally, the *nihil obstat* of the Archbishop of Breslau, Cardinal Bertram, and a by now more relaxed climate cleared the way for his nomination as professor of New Testament in the theology department of the University of Breslau in 1924. When the department was abolished in 1945, he and a few colleagues came to Munich. It was thus that he eventually became my teacher.

The wound that Maier had received in 1912 had never fully healed, even though he could now teach his subject practically without restrictions and was supported by the enthusiasm of his students, to whom he had the gift of communicating his enthusiasm for the New Testament and its proper understanding. Occasionally reminiscences of the period around 1912 would find their way into his lectures. One thing that most impressed itself upon me was a statement that he probably made around 1948 or 1949. He remarked that he was now perfectly at liberty to follow his conscience as a historian, but that the real freedom of exegesis of which he dreamed lay still in the future. He also felt that he would probably not live to see its dawning, but he wished that he might at least be allowed, like

Moses on Mount Nebo, to gaze upon the Promised Land of an exegesis liberated from every shackle of magisterial surveillance. At the time, we sensed that this learned man, who led a compelling priestly life inspired by the faith of the Church, was not only scarred by the decree of the Consistorial Congregation that affected him personally. He also saw the various decrees of the Biblical Commission — for example on the Mosaic authorship of the Pentateuch (1906: EB 181-184), on the historicity of the first three chapters of Genesis (1909: EB 324-331), on the authorship and time of composition of the Psalms (1910: EB 332-339), on Mark and Luke (1912: EB 390-398), on the Synoptic question (1912: EB 399-400), and so forth — as fetters that unduly impeded his work as an exegete.

Maier still felt that such magisterial judgments held Catholic exegetes back from unfettered scholarship, so that Catholic exegesis, in contrast to its Protestant counterpart, was not really up to the latest standards and its scholarly seriousness was in some respects rightly suspect to Protestants. Needless to say, he was also influenced by the belief that rigorous historical work could reliably ascertain the objective data of history, indeed, that it is the only method for obtaining certain knowledge of history and for understanding the meaning of the biblical books — which after all are historical ones — on their own terms. Maier never entertained the slightest doubt about the reliability and unambiguity of the historical method; it never occurred to him that philosophical presuppositions also entered into, and influenced, historical method, and that there could be a need for reflection on the philosophical implications of this method. Like many of his colleagues, he regarded philosophy as a nuisance that could only muddy the pure objectivity of historical scholarship. By the same token, he never felt the pressure of the hermeneutical question — the question, that is, of how the interior situation of the questioner plays a role in shaping his access to a text, so that it is first necessary to get clear about the right way to question and about the means to purify one's questioning. Mount Nebo, then, would surely have held many surprises in store for him, surprises that lay completely beyond the range of his vision.

I would now like to try to climb Mount Nebo with him, as it were, and to survey the country that we have traversed in the last fifty years from the perspective as it looked then. It may be useful for this undertaking to recall the experiences of Moses. Chapter 34 of Deuteronomy describes Moses being allowed to peer from Mount Nebo into the Promised Land, whose whole extent he is able to take in with his eyes. What he is granted is, so to say, a purely geographical view, not a historical one. One could say, however, that chapter 28 of the same book represents a panoramic view, not of geography, but of the future history in and with the land, and that it records a much less consoling glimpse from Mount Nebo. There we read that "the Lord will scatter you among all the peoples, from one end of the earth to the other. . . . Amongst these nations you will find no rest. There will be no place for you to set your foot" (Deut 28:64f.). What Moses saw in this inner vision could be summed up by saying that freedom can destroy itself. When freedom loses its inner measure, it does away with itself.

What, then, might a historical look from Mount Nebo into the land of the last fifty years of exegesis be able to perceive? First of all, a lot that Maier would have found consoling: as it were, the fulfillment of his dream. As early as 1943, the encyclical *Divino Afflante Spiritu* had already introduced a new vision of the relationship between the Magisterium and the scholarly requirements of a historical reading of the Bible. The 1960s represent — to remain with our metaphor — the entrance into the Promised Land of exegetical freedom. The first milestone on this path is the instruction of the Biblical Commission of 21 April 1964 concerning the historical truth of the gospels.[2] The most important milestone, however, is the conciliar Constitution on divine revelation, *Dei Verbum*, whose publication in 1965 truly turned over a new leaf in the relationship between the Magisterium and scientific exegesis. It is not necessary to detail here the achievement of this fundamental text. It begins by defining the concept of Revelation, which is necessary in that Revelation is not simply identical with its written testimony, the Bible. It thereby opens the broad horizon, at once historical and theological, in which biblical interpretation takes place. Such interpretation sees in the biblical writings, not just human books, but testimony to God's own speech. This provides a point of reference for defining the concept of tradition, which likewise extends beyond Scripture, while having Scripture as its center, since Scripture itself is primarily and essentially "tradition." This

2. EB 644-59.

leads then to the third chapter, which deals with the interpretation of Scripture. On the one hand, chapter three impressively lays out the full claim of the historical method to be an indispensable component of the labor of exegesis. On the other hand, however, it also goes on to highlight the properly theological dimension of interpretation — a dimension that, as was said above, is essential if this book is more than the words of human beings.

Let us continue on our journey from Mount Nebo. Maier would surely have rejoiced in a special way over what happened in June 1971. With his Motu Proprio *Sedula Cura*,[3] Paul VI totally restructured the Biblical Commission, so that it was no longer an organ of the Magisterium, but a meeting place for the Magisterium and exegetes: a place of dialogue in which representatives of the Magisterium and outstanding exegetes come together in order, so to say, to find together the intrinsic measure of freedom, which prevents it from destroying itself, and so raises it to the level of true freedom in the first place. Maier would also have been able to experience the joy of seeing one of his most prominent students, Rudolf Schnackenburg, become a member not of the Biblical Commission itself, but of the no less important International Theological Commission, so that he now found himself, as it were, almost a part of that Commission that had once given him so much grief.

Let us mention one more important date, which could be distantly glimpsed from our hypothetical Nebo: the 1993 document of the Pontifical Biblical Commission, *The Interpretation of the Bible in the Church*, in which it is no longer the Magisterium that imposes norms on exegetes from above, but exegetes themselves who attempt to define the criteria that must guide methods of objective interpretation of this special book. Seen purely from the outside, the Bible amounts to nothing more than literature, a collection of writings originating over roughly a millennium: only the common subject from which this literature was born — the pilgrim People of God — makes *one* book out of this collection of literature in all its variety and external contradictions. This people know, in their turn, that their speech and action do not proceed simply from themselves, but owe their existence to the One who creates them as a people: the living God himself.

3. EB 722-39.

Has the dream been fulfilled, then? Have the second fifty years of the Biblical Commission revoked, and set aside as unjust, what the first fifty years had produced? As to the first question, I would say that the dream has been made a reality, even as it has also been corrected in the process. There is no such thing as the pure objectivity of historical method. Philosophy, or the prior hermeneutical question, simply cannot be ruled out. Even in Maier's lifetime, Bultmann's commentary on John, to take just one example, made this clear. Heidegger's philosophy serves Bultmann not only as a vehicle for making historically distant realities present, as a sort of transporter that moves what was once the case into the realm of our today, but also as the pathway that leads us into the text in the first place. Now, Bultmann's project proved to be a failure, but the fact that there is no such thing as a purely historical method — not even in secular literature — has become evident.[4]

It is perfectly understandable that, in the days when the decisions of the then Pontifical Biblical Commission prevented them from a clean application of the historical-critical method, Catholic theologians should cast envious glances at their Protestant colleagues, just as the latter's serious scholarly research was enabling them to publish entirely new discoveries concerning the growth process of this piece of literature that we call the Bible along the journey of the People of God in history. But in all this they did not sufficiently perceive that Protestant theology was experiencing the reverse problem as well. This fact becomes clearly visible, for example, in the lecture on the ecclesial responsibility of theology students delivered in 1936 by Bultmann's great disciple Heinrich Schlier, who later converted to Catholicism.[5] German Protestant Christianity was at the time embroiled in the life-or-death struggle between, on the one hand, the so-called Ger-

---

4. On the methodological and hermeneutical problems being discussed here, see I. de la Potterie et al., *L'esegesi cristiana oggi* (see above, p. 21 n. 29); M. Reiser, "Bibel und Kirche," in *TThZ* 108 (1999): 62-81; idem, "Allegorese und Metaphorik. Vorüberlegungen zu einer Erneuerung der Väterhermeneutik," in F. Sedlmeier, ed., *Gottes Wege suchend. Beiträge zum Verständnis der Bibel und ihrer Botschaft* (Festschrift für Rudolf Mosis zum 70. Geburtstag) (Würzburg: Echter, 2003), pp. 433-65; P. Grech, "La reinterpretazione intrabiblica e l'ermeneutica moderna," in *StPat* 49 (2002): 641-62.

5. H. Schlier, *Der Geist und die Kirche* (Freiburg: Herder, 1980), pp. 225-40.

man Christians, who subordinated Christianity to the ideology of National Socialism, and so falsified its very core, and the Confessing Church, on the other. In this context, Schlier addressed these words to students of theology:

> Consider for a moment which is better: that the Church, in an orderly manner and after mature deliberation, should withdraw the license to teach from the theologian on account of false doctrine, or that the individual should take it upon himself to roam around denouncing this or that theologian as a false teacher and warning against him. After all, one must not suppose that people stop condemning when they are allowed to judge as they see fit. In this area, the only consistent opinion is the liberal one, according to which there is no such thing as a decisive judgment concerning the truth of doctrine in the first place, and that therefore every doctrine has a little bit of truth and is to be tolerated in the Church. But we do not share this opinion. For it denies that God has truly decided amongst us.[6]

Those who recall that at the time the Protestant faculties of theology were to a large extent almost entirely in the hands of the German Christians, and that Schlier was obliged to leave academic theology on account of the kinds of statements that I just cited, will be able to see the other side of the problem.[7]

---

6. Schlier, *Der Geist und die Kirche*, p. 232.

7. Another aspect of the problem of Church and exegesis within Protestantism comes to light in the autobiographical work of a student of Maier's from his Breslau period, an exegete who would later teach in Munich: O. Kuss, *Dankbarer Abschied* (München: TUDUV-Verlagsgesellschaft, 1981 [²1982]). In this work, Kuss recounts that, "on the night before the exercises in preparation for the subdiaconate were to begin," he left the seminary in Breslau and went to Berlin in order to study classical philology and to attend the lectures of the great Protestant theologians who taught there: "Numerous misgivings and doubts, both in fundamentals and in accidentals, had gathered and were now piling up before the decision . . . that was quickly approaching" (p. 20). In addition, "everything, and I really mean everything, that appeared important to the budding 'scholar' had been thought and written by Protestants, for the most part by 'liberal' Protestants" (p. 23). The end result of this study in Berlin was disappointing, however; Kuss eventually returned to the seminary in Breslau and received ordination as a Catholic priest. He adds: "As soon as the 'Church'

We thus come to the second, concluding question. How should we assess the first fifty years of the Biblical Commission today? Was it merely a muzzling of the freedom of theology that we can only consider to be tragic, a mass of errors from which it was necessary to liberate ourselves during the second fifty years of the Commission — or must we not consider this difficult process in a more differentiated fashion? That things are not so simple as they appeared to be in the first flush of enthusiasm following the Council's fresh start should be obvious from what has just been said. It remains correct that by making the judgments that we have mentioned, the Magisterium overextended the range of what faith can guarantee with certainty; and that, as a result, the Magisterium's credibility was injured and the freedom needed for exegetical research and interrogation was unduly narrowed. But it remains equally correct that faith has something to say about matters of scriptural interpretation and that pastors therefore also have the task of offering correctives when exegetes lose sight of the specific nature of this book and an allegedly pure objectivity obscures what is special about, and proper to, Holy Scripture. In this respect, it was indispensable for there to be a process of wrestling over the correct hermeneutics of the Bible and the proper place of historical-critical exegesis.

It seems to me that we can distinguish two levels of the problem that has been at issue. The first level is the question concerning where the purely historical dimension of the Bible ends and where its specificity, which eludes purely historical rationality, begins. Putting it the other way around,

---

became an issue, a situation of conflict also seemed to exist. The professor at the podium . . . for whom the 'Bible' . . . was a book like all other books . . . and the pastor in the pulpit waving the Bible . . . and the interpretation of the Bible in light of the confessional writings . . . — those were two people who hardly seemed to overlap. Gradually I finally came to the . . . realization that the 'Holy Scripture' . . . was in better hands with the audacious confidence of the Roman Catholic Church than under the protection of the seemingly endless variety of options already tried out in the wide world of Protestantism" (pp. 28f.). Tragically, Kuss then lost his faith in the post-conciliar climate where the total freedom of exegesis that he had wished for was dominant; it seemed to him now that the liberal opinion was confirmed, according to which "the Bible is a book like all other books"; he could no longer see "that with the Bible we were dealing with something whose incomparability admitted of no competition, something fundamental" (pp. 28f.). His book is thus the story of his farewell (*Abschied*) to the faith of the Church, to his own past as a Catholic exegete.

we can say that we are dealing with a problem internal to the historical method itself: What is it able to do and what are its inner limits? What other methods of understanding are required for a text of this nature?

The process of intellectual struggle over these issues that had become a necessary task can in a certain sense be compared with the similar process triggered by the Galileo affair. Until Galileo, it had seemed that the geocentric world picture was inextricably bound up with the revealed message of the Bible, and that champions of the heliocentric world picture were destroying the core of Revelation. It became necessary fully to reconceive the relationship between the outward form of presentation and the real message of the whole, and it required a gradual process before the criteria could be elaborated that made it possible to place scientific rationality and the specific message of the Bible in a correct relationship. Of course, the conflict can never be settled once and for all, because the faith attested to by the Bible also involves the material world; the Bible still makes claims about this world — concerning its origin as a whole and man's origin in particular. The reduction of the whole of reality to purely material causes, the banishment of creative spirit to the sphere of pure subjectivity, is incompatible with the basic message of the Bible. This incompatibility commits us, however, to a dispute about the essence of real rationality itself; for if a purely materialistic account of reality presents itself as the only possible expression of rationality, then rationality itself has been misunderstood.

Something analogous can be said with respect to history. At first it seemed as if the ascription of the Pentateuch to Moses or of the gospels to the four individuals whom tradition names as their authors were indispensable conditions of the trustworthiness of Scripture and, therefore, of the faith founded upon it. Here, too, it was necessary for the territories to be re-surveyed, as it were; the basic relationship between faith and history needed to be re-thought. This sort of clarification could not be achieved overnight. The opinion that faith as such has nothing to do with historical facts and must leave their investigation to the historians is Gnosticism. It dis-incarnates the faith and turns it into a pure idea. But precisely the ontological realism of historical events is intrinsically constitutive of the faith that originates from the Bible. A God that cannot intervene in history and show himself in it is not the God of the Bible. For this reason, the reality of

Jesus' birth from the Virgin Mary, the real institution of the Last Supper by Jesus himself, his bodily Resurrection from the dead — the fact that the tomb was empty — are all an element of the faith itself that it can and must defend against supposedly better historical knowledge. The fact that, in all essentials, Jesus was the one whom the gospels show him to be is not a historical conjecture, but is what faith is all about. Objections that aim to persuade us otherwise are not an expression of true scientific knowledge, but are an example of method overestimating itself. That having been said, it is true that many details must remain open and be left to the efforts of responsible exegesis. We have learned this much in the last fifty years.

With that, the second level of the problem begins to appear. What is at stake is not simply a catalog of indispensable historical elements of the faith. The issue concerns the scope of reason and the basis of the rationality of faith and the faithfulness of reason. After all, the last fifty years have not brought only a correction of earlier judgments by which the Biblical Commission overreached its competence in purely historical matters. They have also taught us new things about the method and limits of historical knowledge. Heisenberg's uncertainty principle shows in the domain of the physical sciences that our knowledge is never a mere reproduction of objective reality, but is also shaped by the participation of the subject, the starting point of his questioning, and his perceptive capacities. This is, of course, true to a much greater extent when man himself is in play and, *a fortiori*, where the mystery of God comes within our ken. In this sense, neither faith and science, nor Magisterium and exegesis, need be juxtaposed any longer like two self-contained worlds. Faith is itself a way of knowing; the attempt to set it aside does not produce pure objectivity, but sets up a cognitive standpoint that rules out a certain perspective and refuses to acknowledge the contingency of the conditions of the vision it itself has opted for. By contrast, when we realize that the Holy Scriptures come from a subject that is still very much alive — the pilgrim People of God — it is clear, even rationally, that this subject has something to contribute to the understanding of this book.

The Promised Land of freedom is more thrilling and many-sided than an exegete like Maier could have imagined in 1948. The intrinsic conditions of freedom have clearly emerged. Freedom requires keen listening, awareness of the limits of individual methods, and the full seriousness of *ratio*. But it also requires a willingness to be modest and to transcend one's own perspective, in communion with the thought and life of the subject that vouches for the unity of the manifold writings of the Old and New Testament as one work — precisely as Holy Scripture. We are profoundly grateful for the openings that Vatican II has given us as the fruit of a long struggle. But we also refuse simply to condemn what went before, but see it as a necessary part of the process of knowing, which will always challenge us anew on account of the magnitude of the Word spoken to us and of the limits of our capabilities. But that is just what is so beautiful. And so, after one hundred years of the Biblical Commission, and in spite of all the problems that have fallen within these hundred years, we can look forward to our future path with gratitude and hope.

Translated by Adrian Walker

Original Publications

We are grateful to all the authors and publishing houses for having facilitated the texts and necessary permissions that we might go forward with this publication — in particular to the Libreria Editrice Vaticana that, in the name of Pope Benedict XVI, has authorized us to publish his two contributions. Our thanks go also to Cardinal Albert Vanhoye — who provided us with the original, unedited French text — for his collaborative efforts and for personally reviewing our English translation; also Fr. Klemens Stock and Prof. Bruna Costacurta have had the kindness to review the version of their articles.

Ratzinger, J., "Schriftauslegung im Widerstreit. Zur Frage nach Grundlagen und Weg der Exegese heute," in J. Ratzinger, ed., *Schriftauslegung im Widerstreit* (QD, 117) (Freiburg/Basel/Wien: Herder, 1989), pp. 15-44.[1]

1. Original publication: "Biblical Interpretation in Crisis: On the Question of the Foundations and Approaches of Exegesis Today," in R. J. Neuhaus, ed., *Biblical Interpretation in Crisis: The Ratzinger Conference on Bible and Church* (Grand Rapids: Eerdmans, 1989), pp. 1-23. Italian version: "L'interpretazione biblica in conflitto," in I. de la Potterie, R. Guardini, J. Ratzinger, G. Colombo, and E. Bianchi, *L'esegesi cristiana oggi* (Casale Monferrato: Piemme, 1991 [³2000]), pp. 93-125. French version: "L'interprétation de la Bible en conflit," in R. Guardini, H. de Lubac, H. Urs von Balthasar, J. Ratzinger, and I. de la Potterie, *L'exégèse chrétienne aujourd'hui* (Paris: Fayard, 2000), pp. 65-109. All the articles

De la Potterie, I., "L'exégèse biblique, science de la foi," in R. Guardini, H. de Lubac, H. Urs von Balthasar, J. Ratzinger, and I. de la Potterie, *L'exégèse chrétienne aujourd'hui* (Paris: Fayard, 2000), pp. 111-60.[2]

Beauchamp, P., "È possibile una teologia biblica?" in G. Angelini, ed., *La rivelazione attestata. La Bibbia fra testo e teologia* (Raccolta di studi in onore del Cardinale C. M. Martini) (Milano: Glotta, 1998), pp. 319-32.

Costacurta, B., "Esegesi e lettura credente della Scrittura," in *Gregorianum* 73 (1992): 739-45.

Stock, K., "Christus in der heutigen Exegese. Standortbestimmung und Ausblick," in *Geist und Leben* 59 (1986): 215-28.[3]

Vanhoye, A., "La parola di Dio nella vita della Chiesa: La recezione della 'Dei Verbum,'" in R. Fisichella, ed., *Il Concilio Vaticano II. Recezione e attualità alla luce del Giubileo*, Cinisello Balsamo (Milano: Paoline, 2000), pp. 29-45.

Ratzinger, J., "Kirchliches Lehramt und Exegese," in *Communio.de* 32 (2003): 522-29.

---

published in this book have previously received a Spanish version in the book *Escritura e interpretación. Los fundamentos de la interpretación bíblica* (edición y prólogo de L. Sánchez Navarro y C. Granados) (LP 42; Madrid: Ediciones Palabra, 2003; [2]2005).

2. Italian version: "L'esegesi biblica, scienza della fede," in *L'esegesi cristiana oggi* (o.c.), pp. 127-65.

3. English version: "Christ in Contemporary Exegesis: Where We Are and Where We Are Going," in *Communio.en* 30 (2003): 463-77. In our book Fr. Stock offers an updated version of his work.

Index of Holy Scripture

Index of Magisterial and Ecclesial Documents

Index of Magisterial and Ecclesial Documents

Index of Authors

Index of Subjects

Index of Subjects

Gospel, xxii, 15, 46-47, 49, 57, 64, 68-70, 73, 88-93, 96-103, 108-9, 129, 134-35

Hellenization, 14-16, 88
Historical-critical method, xii-xvi, xix-xx, 1-20, 28-29, 32-33, 42, 79-81, 88-93, 123-24, 131, 133
Historicism, 54

Incarnation, xviii, 23, 134-35
Inerrancy, 42-44
Inspiration, xviii, 38-48, 110, 115-19, 122, 125

Jesusbewegung, 69
Judaism, 14-15, 68-69, 91

Kerygma, 16, 46

Lectio divina, 119, 124
Liberationist exegesis, 90-91
Literary genres, 5, 36, 57, 81, 120
Liturgy, 70-71
Locutio Dei, 106, 109

Magisterium, xv, 43, 105, 126-36
Materialistic interpretation, 4-5, 90, 134
Mystery of Scripture, 20, 39-41, 44-51, 61-62, 76-77, 86, 103, 115-16, 135
Myth, 5, 11, 14, 16, 19, 88

Narrative act, xiv-xv, 75-77, 124

Philology, xviii, 28, 32-33, 35-37, 40, 45, 51-55, 58-59, 80, 121
Physiologein, 20
Positivism, 8, 31-32, 58, 64
Pre/Post-paschal, 11-12, 87-88, 92
Providentissimus Deus, xviii, 42, 119-20, 122
Psychological interpretation, 5, 54, 91

Rationalism, 41-42, 53, 113
Religionsgeschichte, 16-17, 88
Rereading, 26, 63, 118
Rhetorical analysis, 82, 92-93, 124

Science, xv, 18, 54-55, 66, 74-75, 111, 120, 123, 129; historical science, xxi, 40, 54, 65, 121; linguistic science, 43-44; literary science, 28-29, 32-33, 40, 50-51, 59, 81; natural science, 8-9, 18, 20-24, 135; religious science, 32; science of faith, 30-64; science of revelation, 59; theological science, 32, 53, 80
Secularization, 32, 45, 63-64, 123
Sitz im Leben, 5, 28, 116
Sociological approach, 89
Source: of the biblical text, 2, 27-28, 32, 83-85, 90, 92; illusion of the sources, 37-38; of revelation, 104, 107-12
Spirit, 73, 98, 100, 115, 120, 125; and inspiration, 45-48, 106, 109, 115-16, 122; and sense of Scripture, 48, 60, 70, 118, 122; Spirit in which Scripture was written, 31, 36, 50, 61-62, 122; and tradition, 62, 109-11
Spirituality, 52
Sympathy, 21, 29
Synchronic method, 28, 80, 83, 85

Teleology, 25
Theology and exegesis, xxi, 2-3, 20-21, 28-29, 32-34, 51-53, 59, 64, 65-78, 119-24
"Third Quest," 89-91
Tradition, xxii, 6, 8, 26, 33-34, 38, 45-46, 53, 56, 62-64, 104-25, 129-30, 134
Truth, 22, 31, 41-47, 51, 57, 60, 63-64, 70, 73, 75, 79-80, 86, 108

Uncertainty principle, 8-9, 135
Unity of Scripture, xiv, xx, xxiii, 6, 12, 25, 41, 48-51, 62, 66-68, 84-85, 93, 122, 124, 136

Index of Subjects